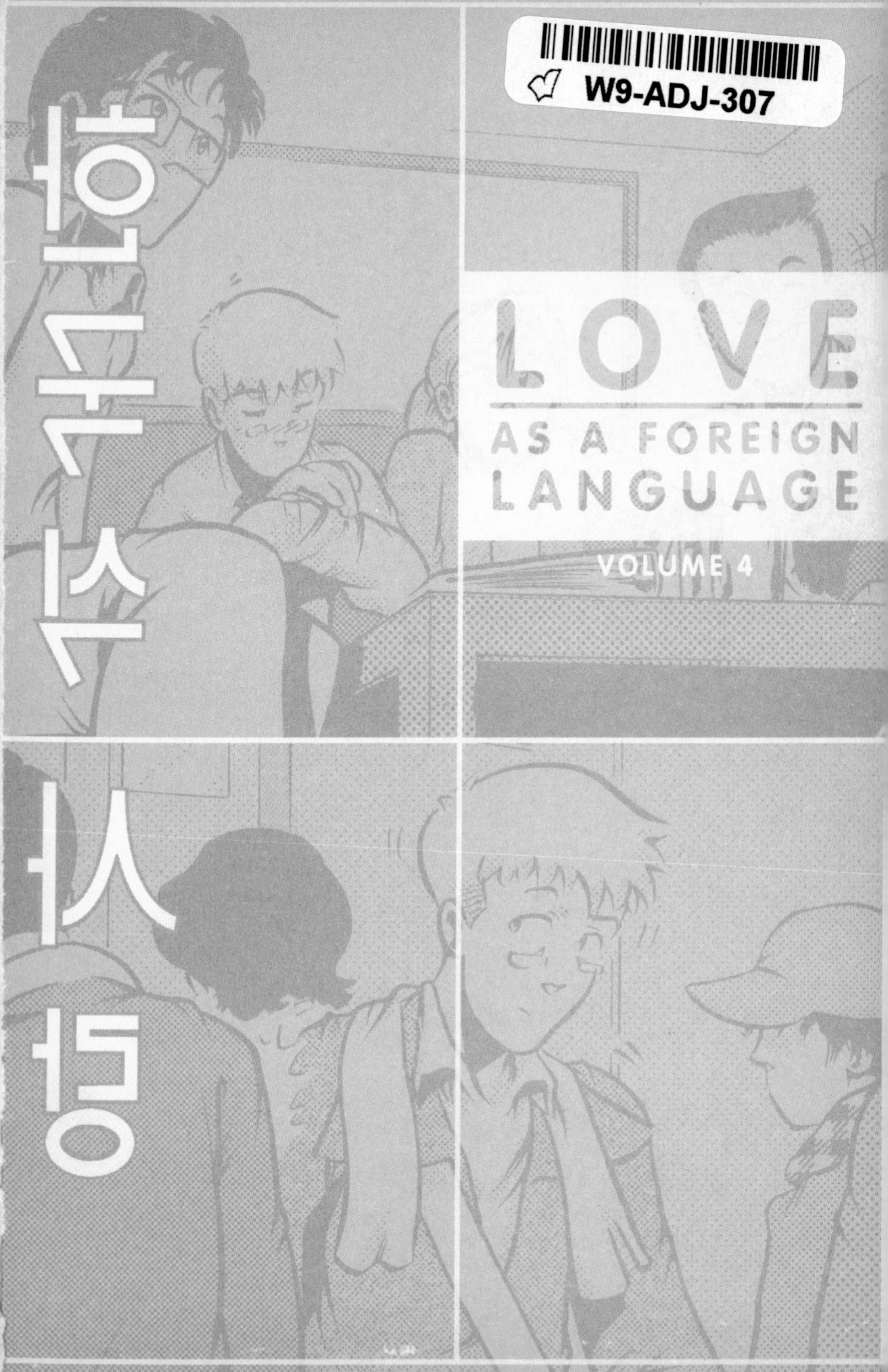

LOVE AS A FOREIGN LANGUAGE

VOLUME 4

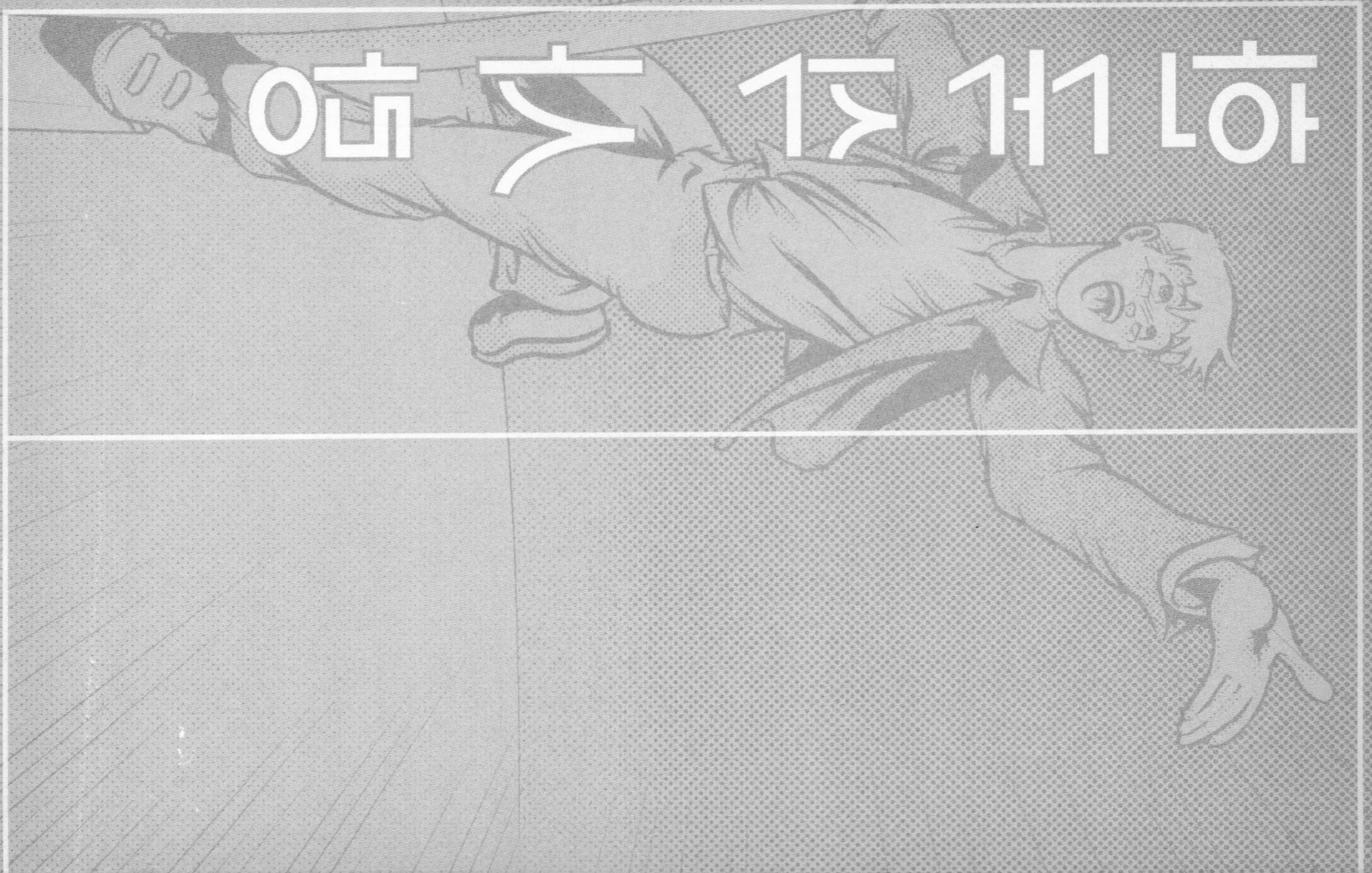

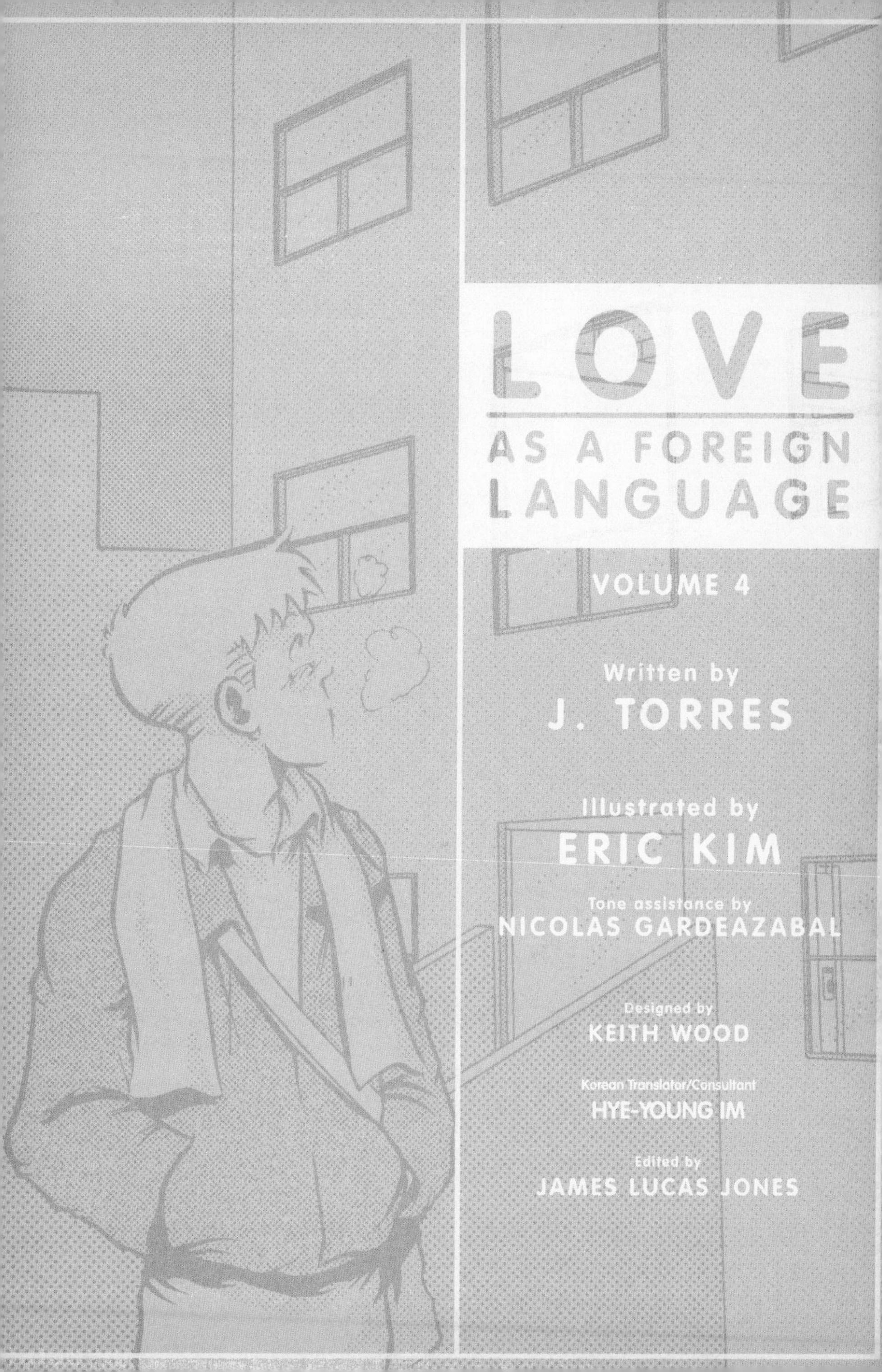

LOVE AS A FOREIGN LANGUAGE

VOLUME 4

Written by
J. TORRES

Illustrated by
ERIC KIM

Tone assistance by
NICOLAS GARDEAZABAL

Designed by
KEITH WOOD

Korean Translator/Consultant
HYE-YOUNG IM

Edited by
JAMES LUCAS JONES

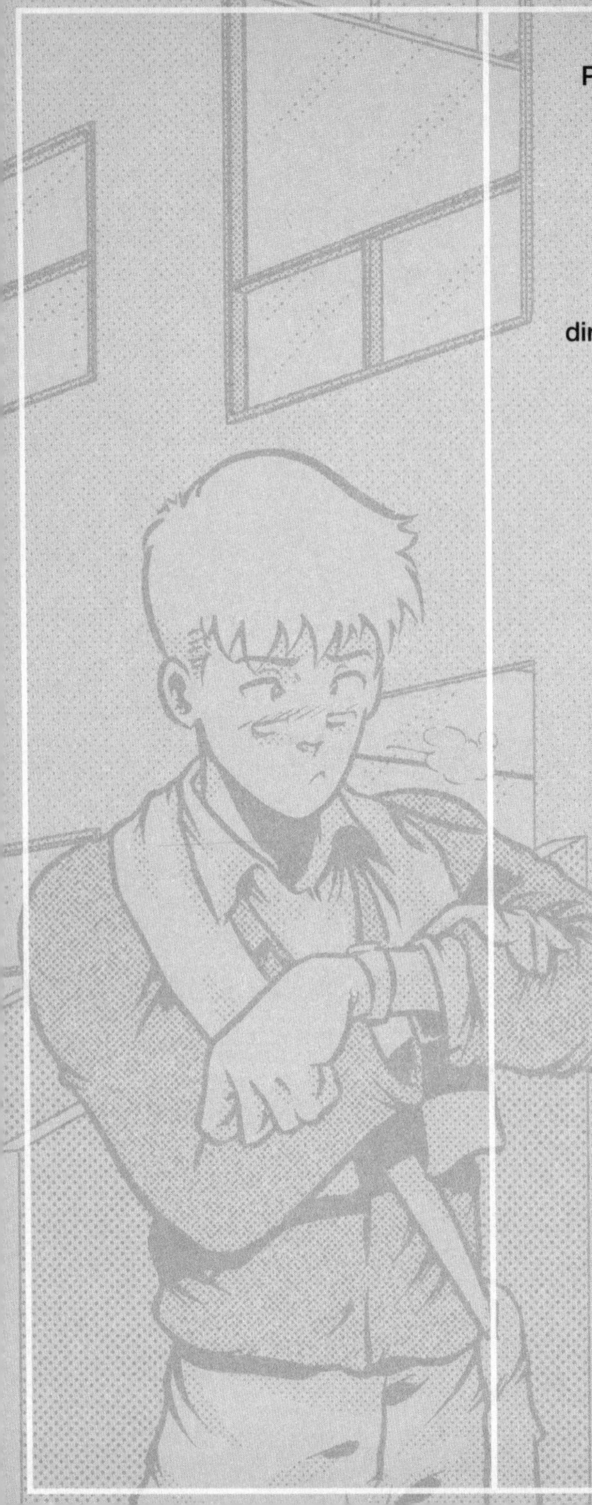

Published by Oni Press, Inc.

publisher
JOE NOZEMACK

managing editor
RANDAL C. JARRELL

director of marketing and sales
MARYANNE SNELL

ONI PRESS, INC.
1305 SE Martin Luther King Blvd.
Suite A
Portland, OR 97214
USA

www.onipress.com
www.jtorresonline.com
www.inkskratch.com

First edition: October 2005
ISBN 1-932664-19-X

1 3 5 7 9 10 8 6 4 2
PRINTED IN CANADA.

Chapter 14

MANWHA WERE YOU THINKING?

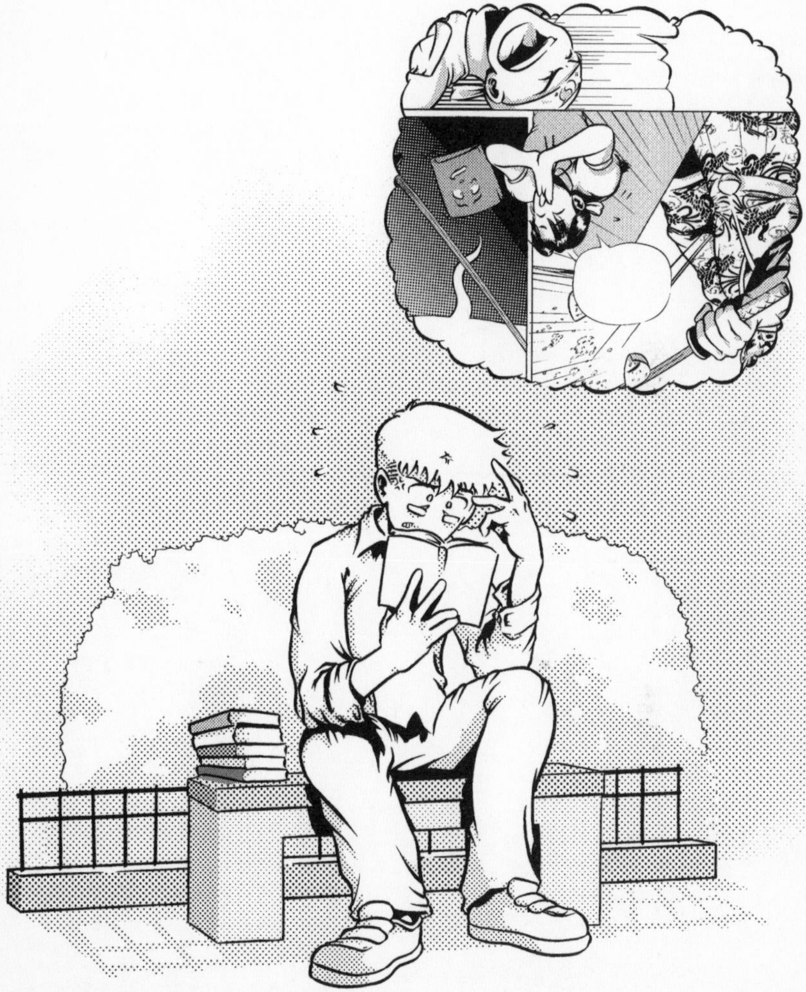

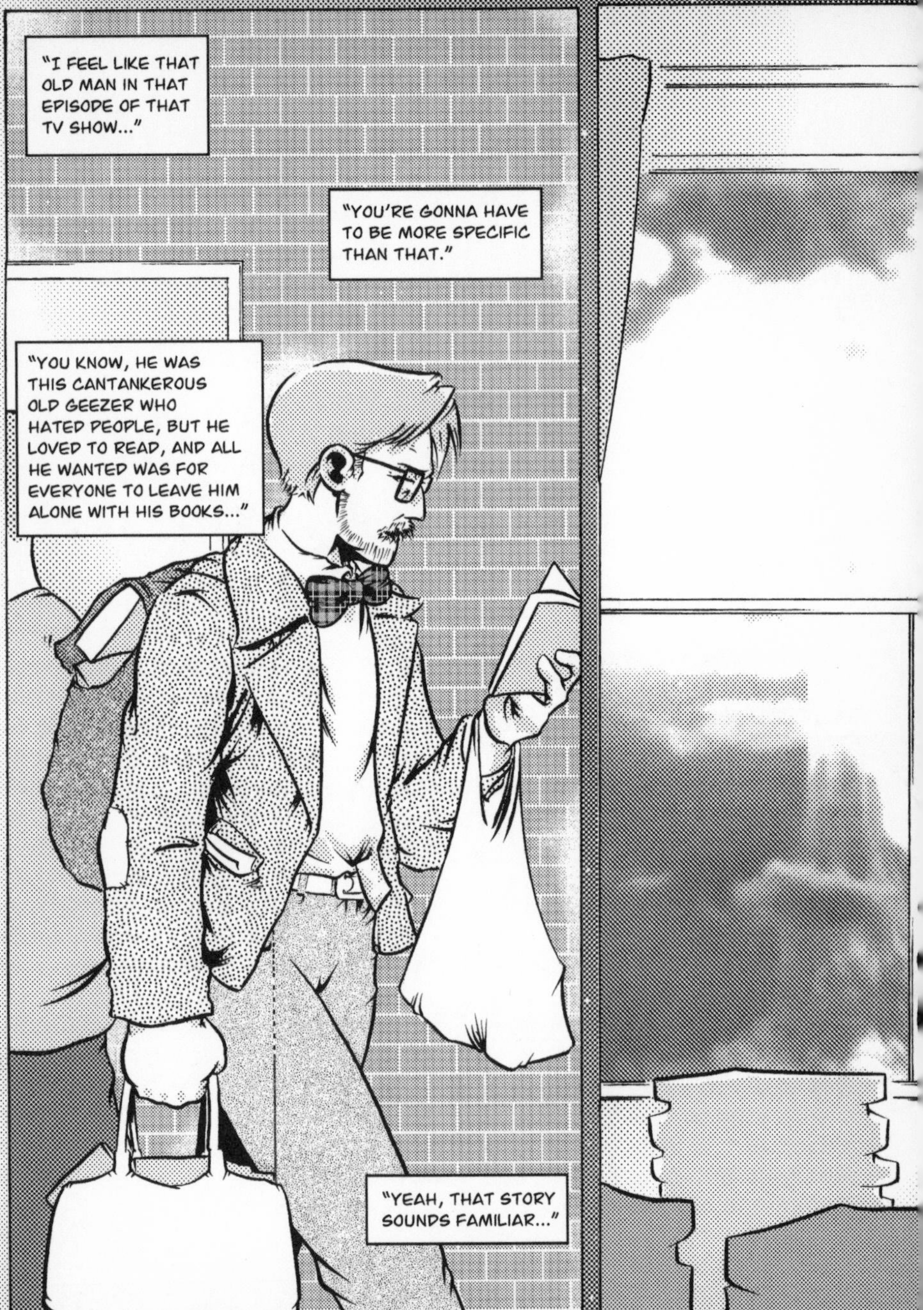
"I FEEL LIKE THAT OLD MAN IN THAT EPISODE OF THAT TV SHOW..."
"YOU'RE GONNA HAVE TO BE MORE SPECIFIC THAN THAT."
"YOU KNOW, HE WAS THIS CANTANKEROUS OLD GEEZER WHO HATED PEOPLE, BUT HE LOVED TO READ, AND ALL HE WANTED WAS FOR EVERYONE TO LEAVE HIM ALONE WITH HIS BOOKS..."
"YEAH, THAT STORY SOUNDS FAMILIAR..."

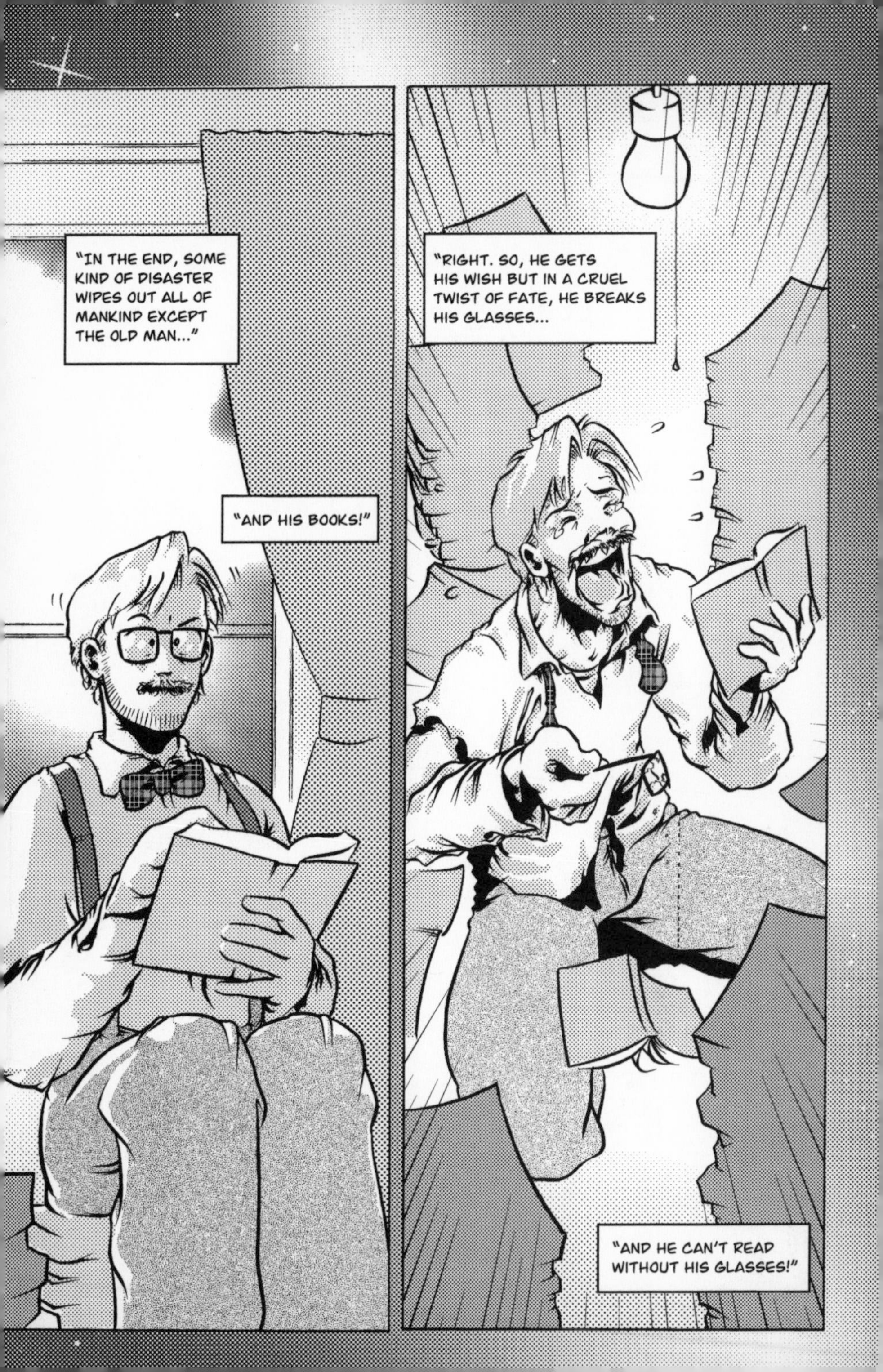
"IN THE END, SOME KIND OF DISASTER WIPES OUT ALL OF MANKIND EXCEPT THE OLD MAN..."
"AND HIS BOOKS!"
"RIGHT. SO, HE GETS HIS WISH BUT IN A CRUEL TWIST OF FATE, HE BREAKS HIS GLASSES...
"AND HE CAN'T READ WITHOUT HIS GLASSES!"

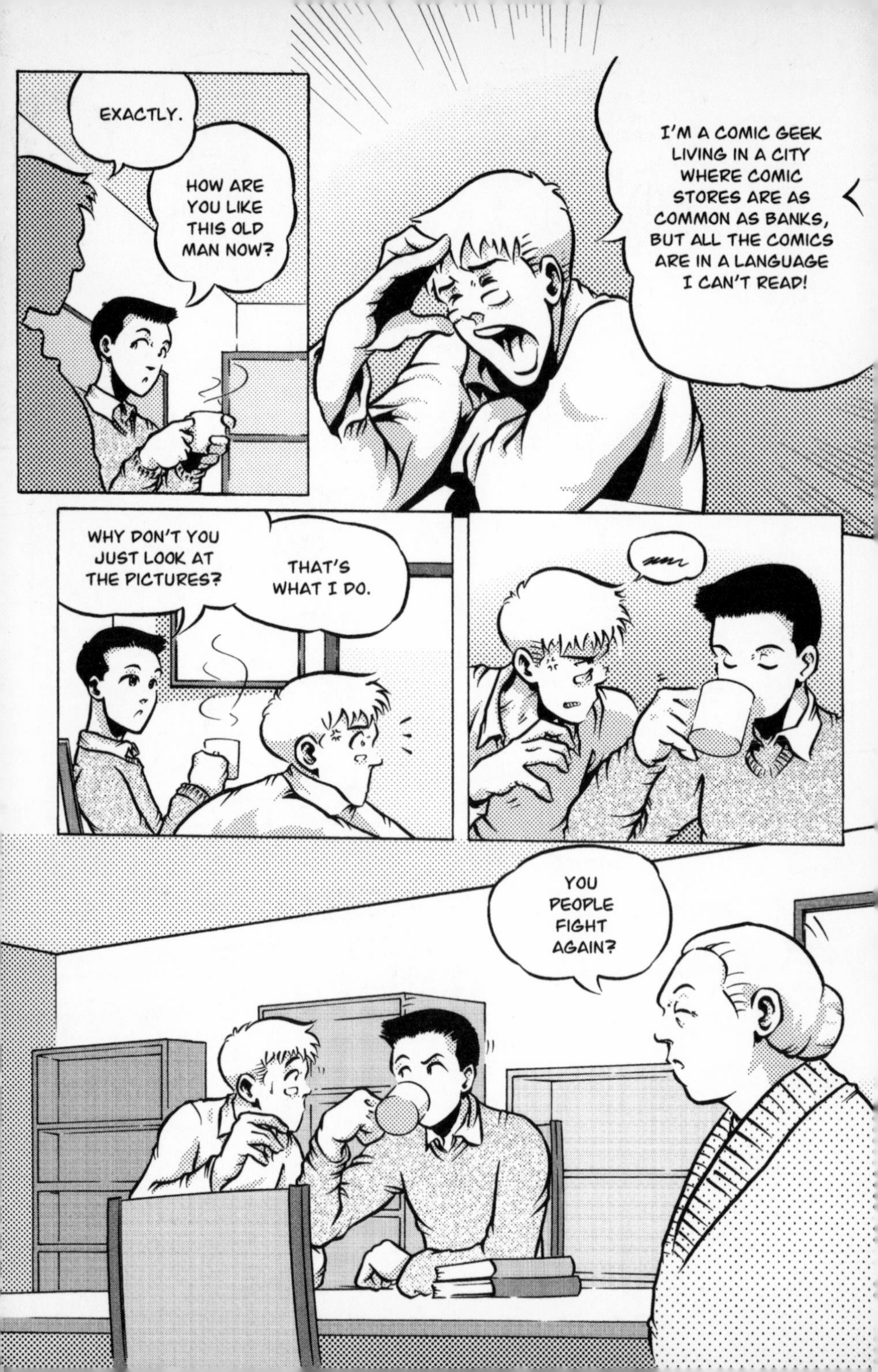
EXACTLY.
HOW ARE YOU LIKE THIS OLD MAN NOW?
I'M A COMIC GEEK LIVING IN A CITY WHERE COMIC STORES ARE AS COMMON AS BANKS, BUT ALL THE COMICS ARE IN A LANGUAGE I CAN'T READ!
WHY DON'T YOU JUST LOOK AT THE PICTURES?
THAT'S WHAT I DO.
YOU PEOPLE FIGHT AGAIN?

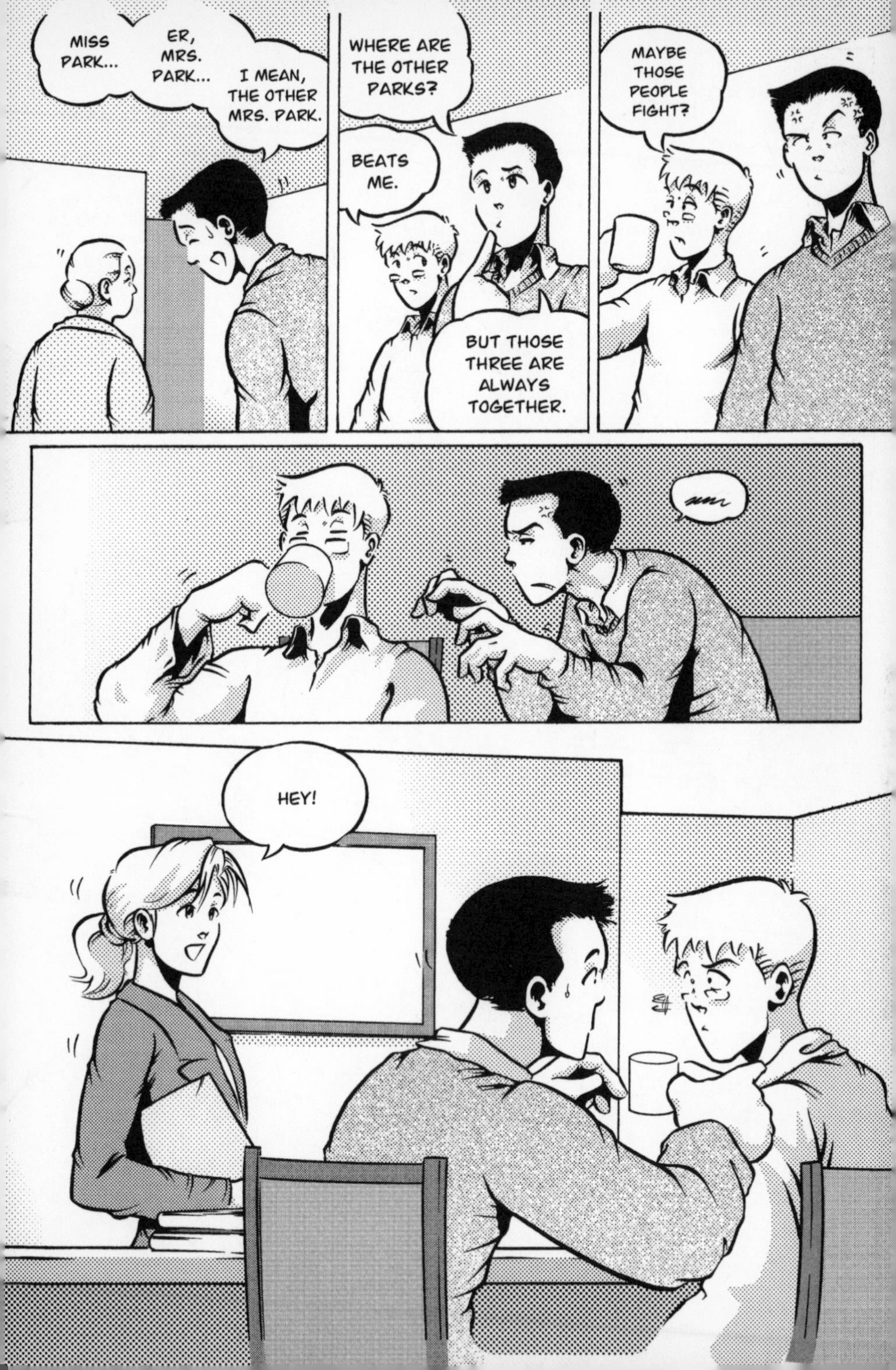
MISS PARK...
ER, MRS. PARK...
I MEAN, THE OTHER MRS. PARK.
WHERE ARE THE OTHER PARKS?
BEATS ME.
BUT THOSE THREE ARE ALWAYS TOGETHER.
MAYBE THOSE PEOPLE FIGHT?
HEY!

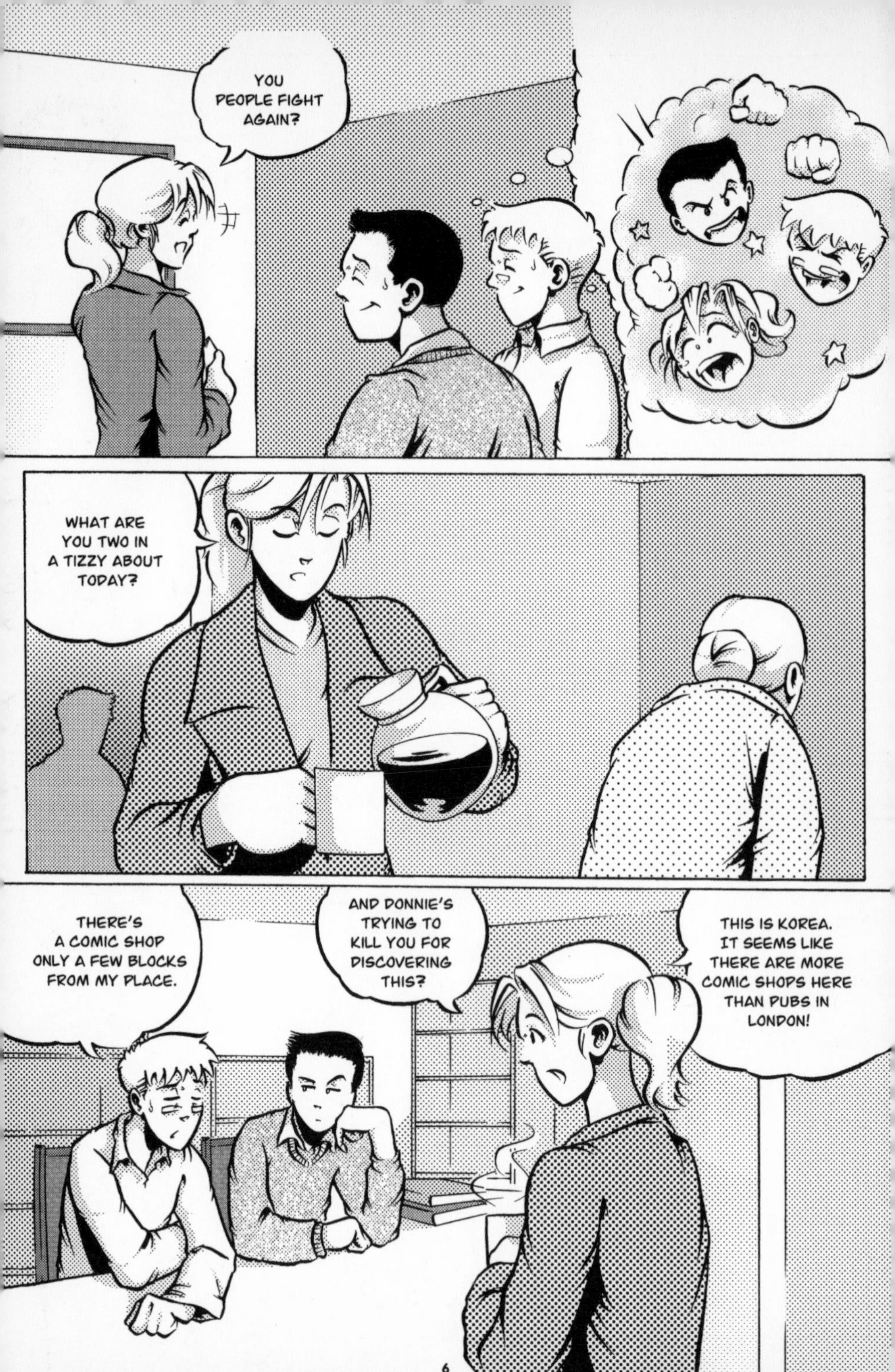
YOU PEOPLE FIGHT AGAIN?
WHAT ARE YOU TWO IN A TIZZY ABOUT TODAY?
THERE'S A COMIC SHOP ONLY A FEW BLOCKS FROM MY PLACE.
AND DONNIE'S TRYING TO KILL YOU FOR DISCOVERING THIS?
THIS IS KOREA. IT SEEMS LIKE THERE ARE MORE COMIC SHOPS HERE THAN PUBS IN LONDON!

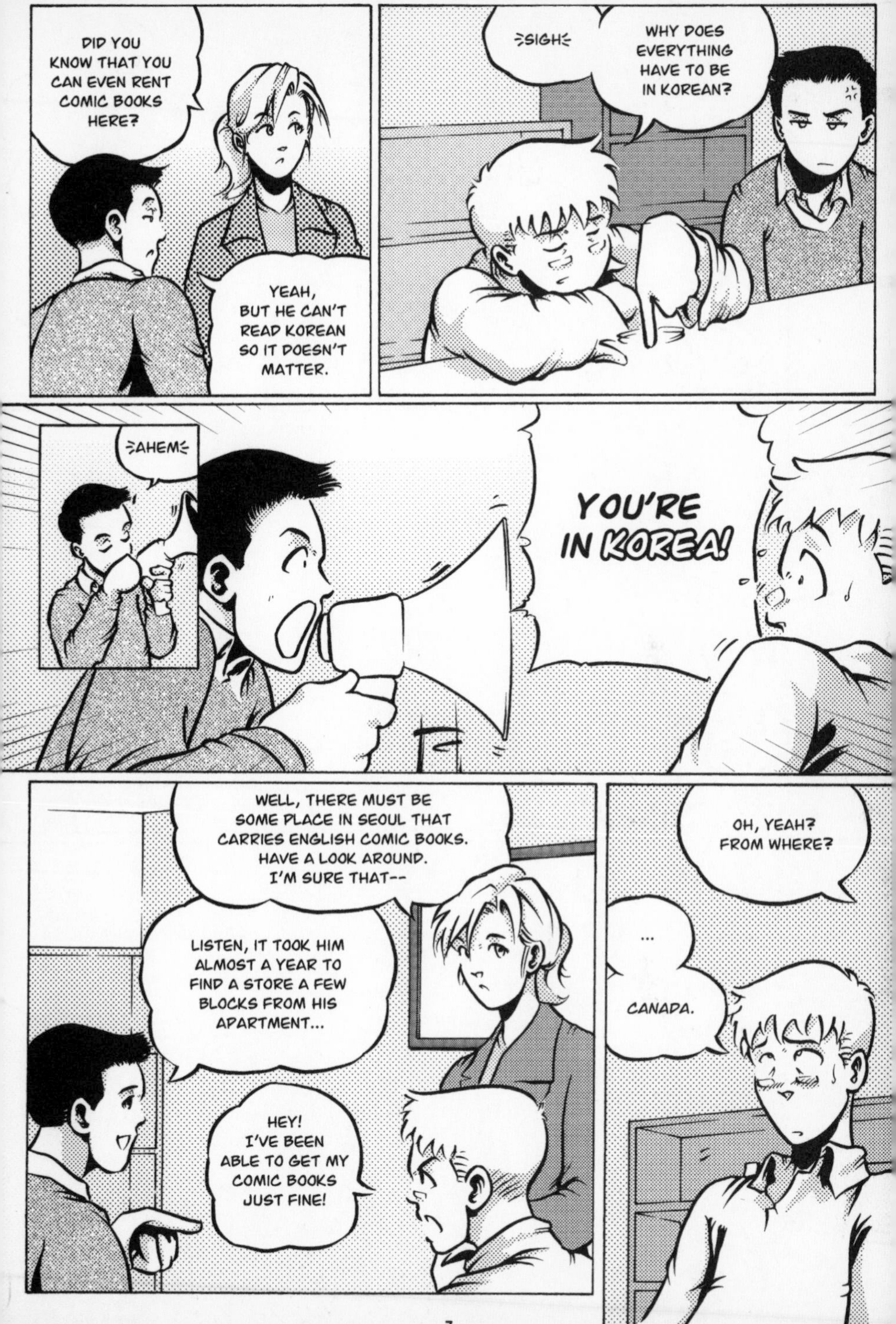

DID YOU KNOW THAT YOU CAN EVEN RENT COMIC BOOKS HERE?
YEAH, BUT HE CAN'T READ KOREAN SO IT DOESN'T MATTER.
≥SIGH≤
WHY DOES EVERYTHING HAVE TO BE IN KOREAN?
≥AHEM≤
YOU'RE IN KOREA!
WELL, THERE MUST BE SOME PLACE IN SEOUL THAT CARRIES ENGLISH COMIC BOOKS. HAVE A LOOK AROUND. I'M SURE THAT--
LISTEN, IT TOOK HIM ALMOST A YEAR TO FIND A STORE A FEW BLOCKS FROM HIS APARTMENT...
HEY! I'VE BEEN ABLE TO GET MY COMIC BOOKS JUST FINE!
OH, YEAH? FROM WHERE?
...
CANADA.

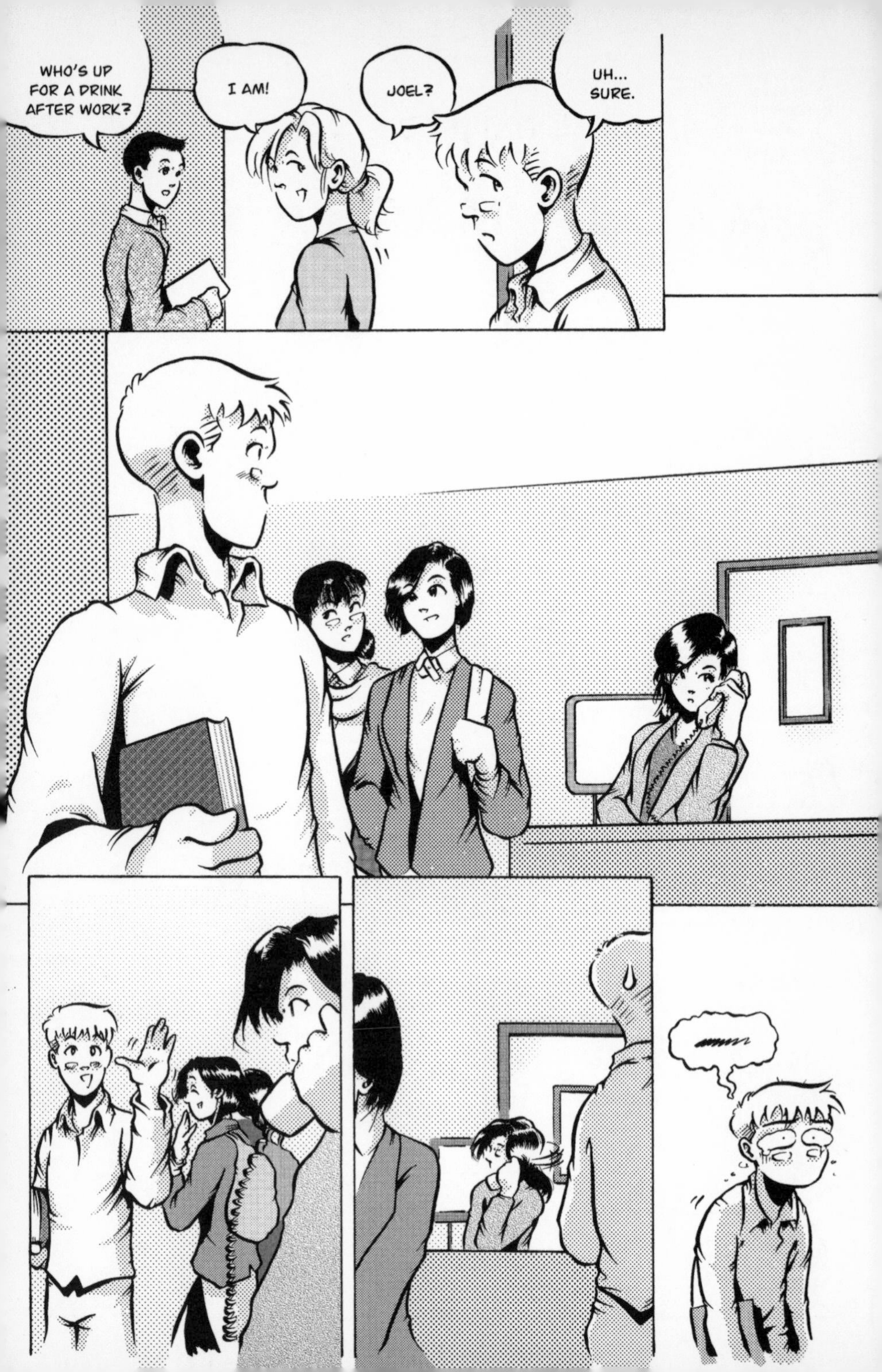

WHO'S UP FOR A DRINK AFTER WORK?
I AM!
JOEL?
UH... SURE.

Chapter 15

MACHA MACHA MAN

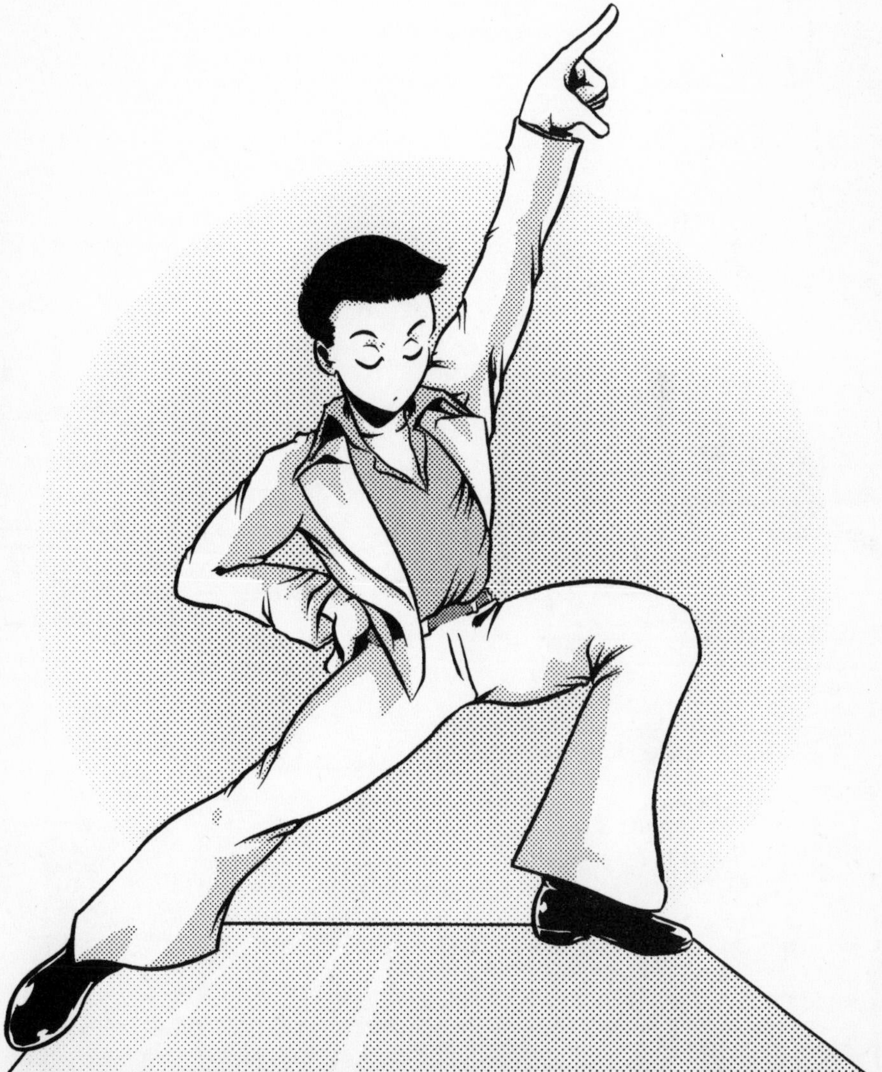

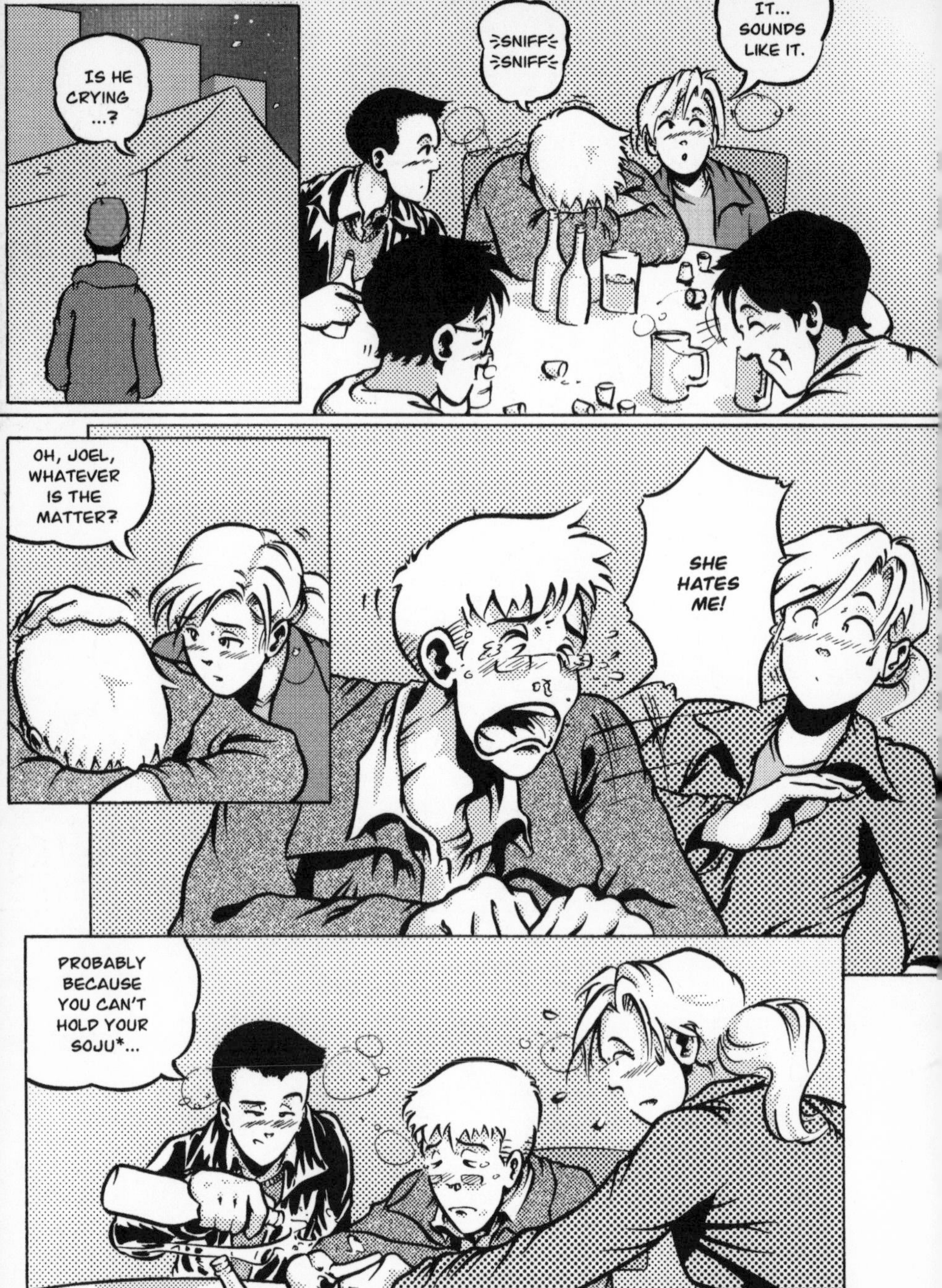
IS HE CRYING ...?
=SNIFF= =SNIFF=
IT... SOUNDS LIKE IT.
OH, JOEL, WHATEVER IS THE MATTER?
SHE HATES ME!
PROBABLY BECAUSE YOU CAN'T HOLD YOUR SOJU*...
*SOJU: KOREAN RICE LIQUOR

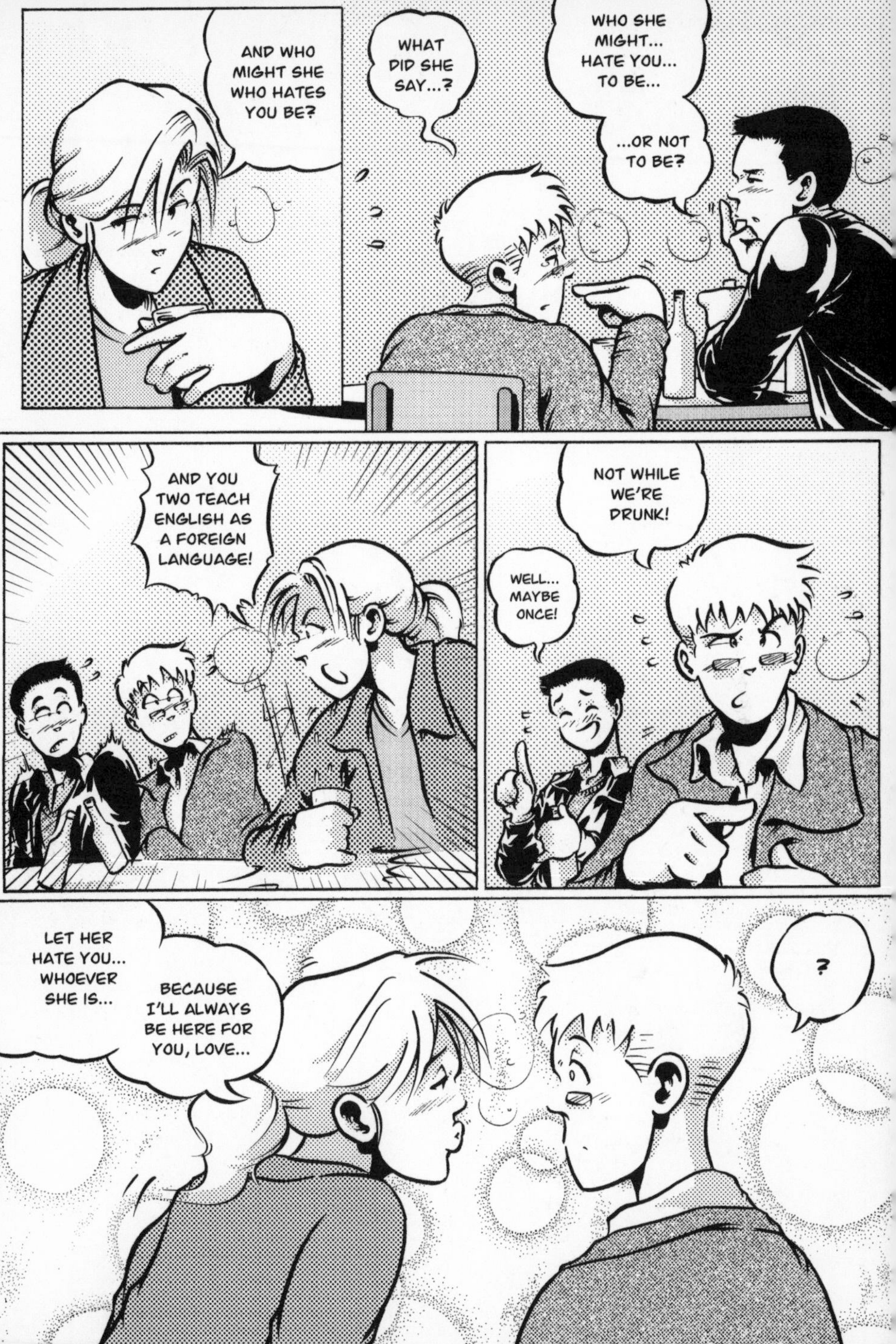
AND WHO MIGHT SHE WHO HATES YOU BE?
WHAT DID SHE SAY...?
WHO SHE MIGHT... HATE YOU... TO BE...
...OR NOT TO BE?
AND YOU TWO TEACH ENGLISH AS A FOREIGN LANGUAGE!
NOT WHILE WE'RE DRUNK!
WELL... MAYBE ONCE!
LET HER HATE YOU... WHOEVER SHE IS...
BECAUSE I'LL ALWAYS BE HERE FOR YOU, LOVE...
?

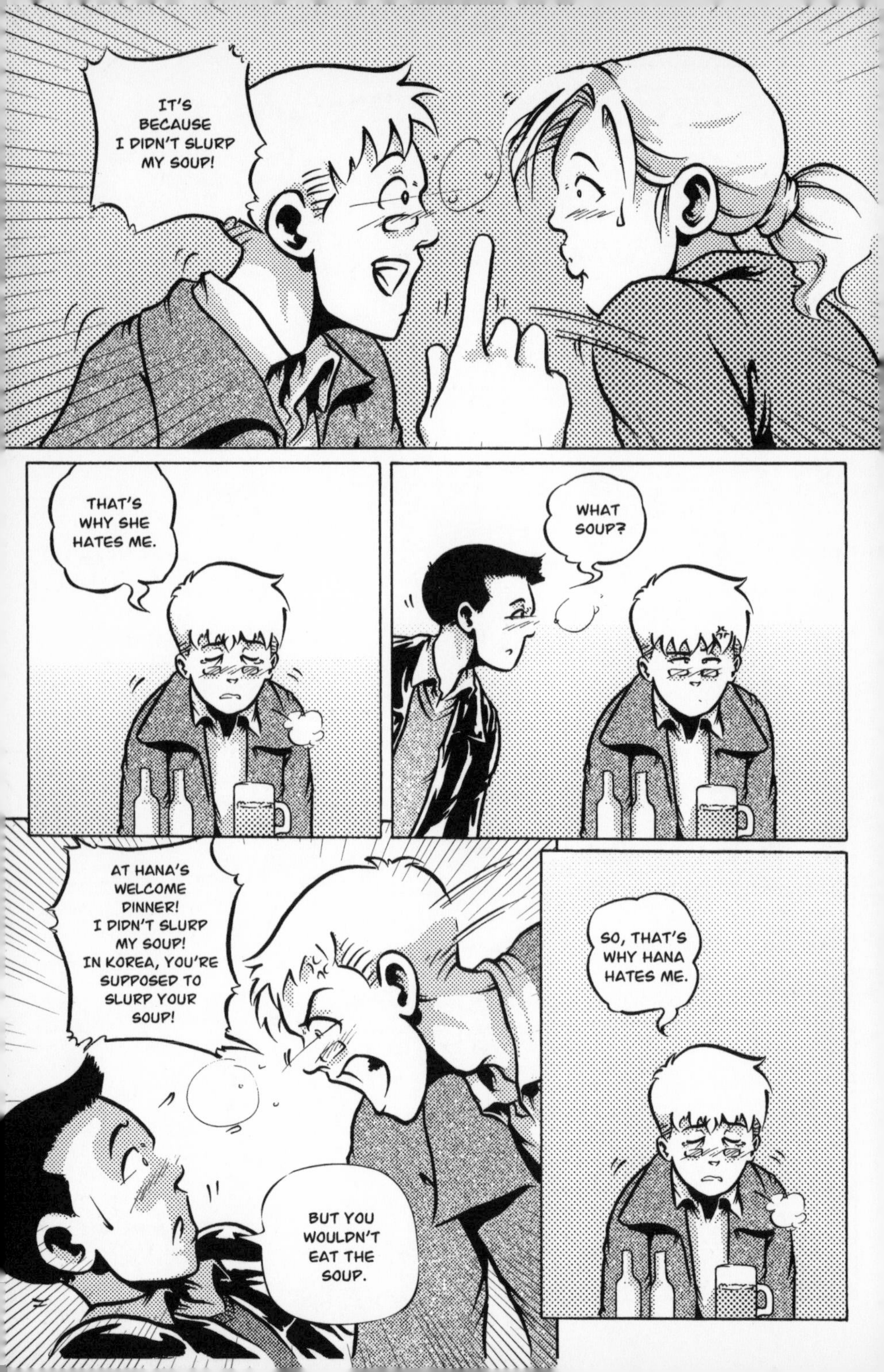
IT'S BECAUSE I DIDN'T SLURP MY SOUP!
THAT'S WHY SHE HATES ME.
WHAT SOUP?
AT HANA'S WELCOME DINNER! I DIDN'T SLURP MY SOUP! IN KOREA, YOU'RE SUPPOSED TO SLURP YOUR SOUP!
BUT YOU WOULDN'T EAT THE SOUP.
SO, THAT'S WHY HANA HATES ME.

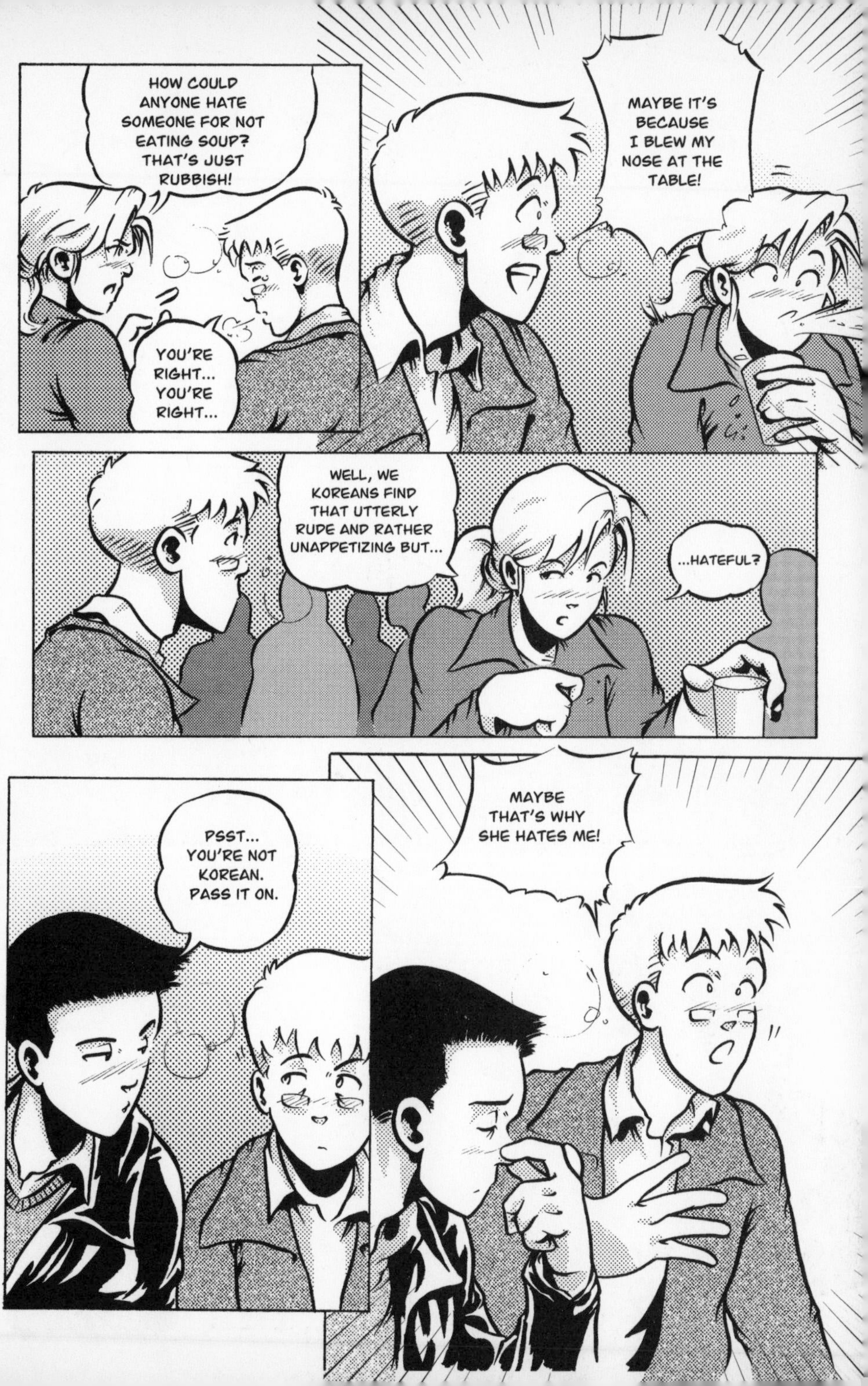
HOW COULD ANYONE HATE SOMEONE FOR NOT EATING SOUP? THAT'S JUST RUBBISH!
YOU'RE RIGHT... YOU'RE RIGHT...
MAYBE IT'S BECAUSE I BLEW MY NOSE AT THE TABLE!
WELL, WE KOREANS FIND THAT UTTERLY RUDE AND RATHER UNAPPETIZING BUT...
...HATEFUL?
MAYBE THAT'S WHY SHE HATES ME!
PSST... YOU'RE NOT KOREAN. PASS IT ON.

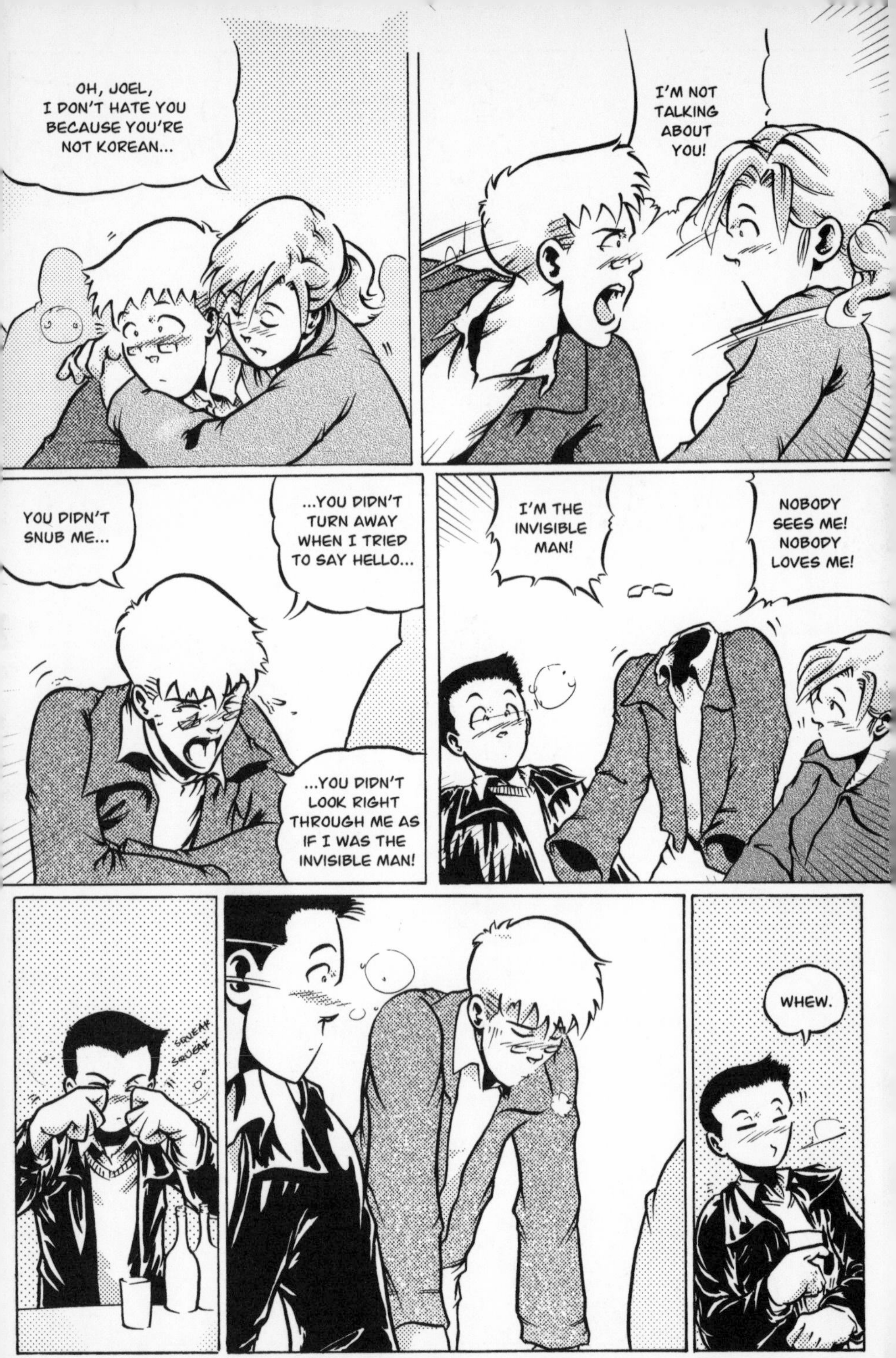
OH, JOEL, I DON'T HATE YOU BECAUSE YOU'RE NOT KOREAN...
I'M NOT TALKING ABOUT YOU!
YOU DIDN'T SNUB ME...
...YOU DIDN'T TURN AWAY WHEN I TRIED TO SAY HELLO...
...YOU DIDN'T LOOK RIGHT THROUGH ME AS IF I WAS THE INVISIBLE MAN!
I'M THE INVISIBLE MAN!
NOBODY SEES ME! NOBODY LOVES ME!
SQUEAK SQUEAK
WHEW.

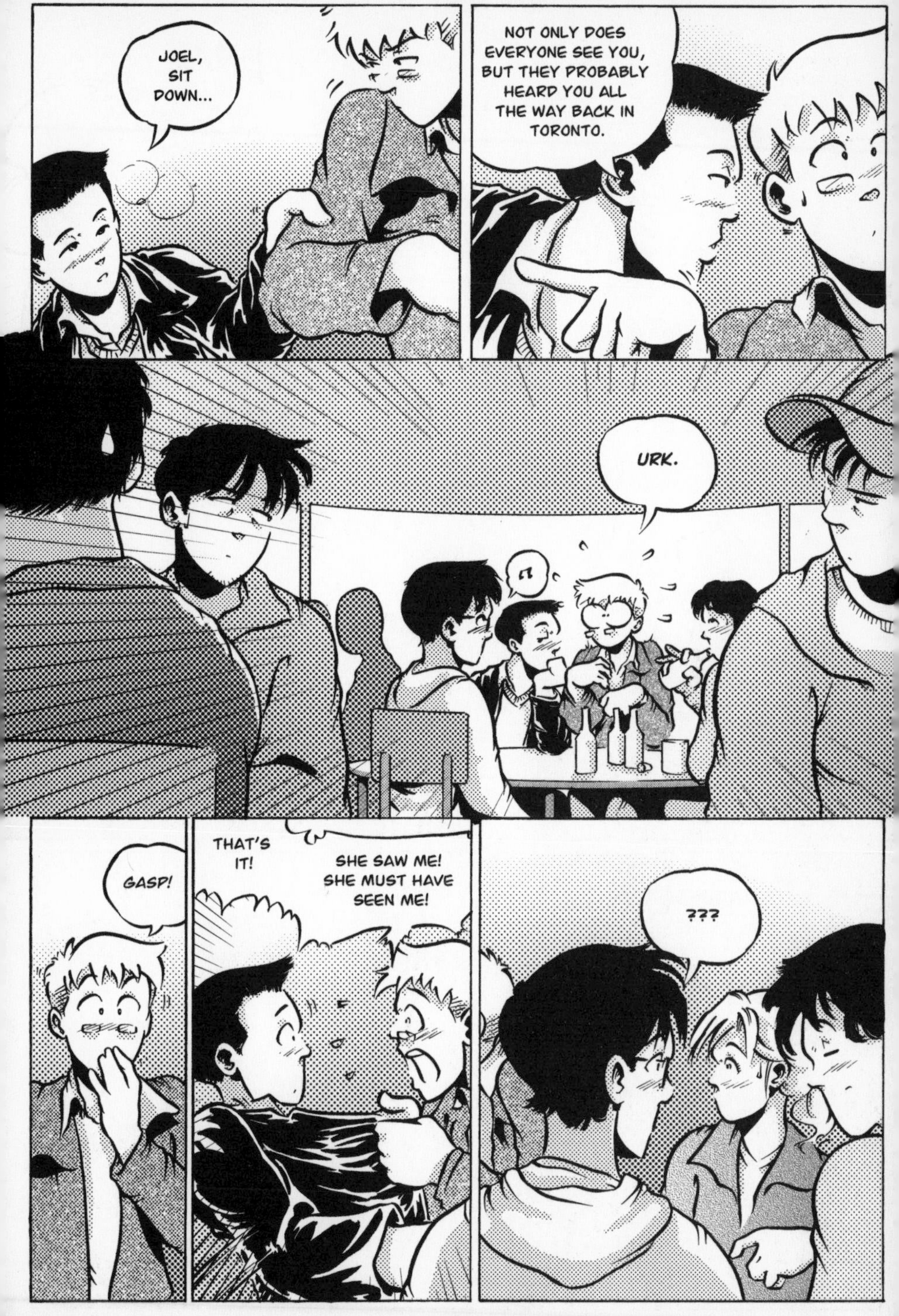
JOEL, SIT DOWN...
NOT ONLY DOES EVERYONE SEE YOU, BUT THEY PROBABLY HEARD YOU ALL THE WAY BACK IN TORONTO.
URK.
GASP!
THAT'S IT!
SHE SAW ME! SHE MUST HAVE SEEN ME!
???

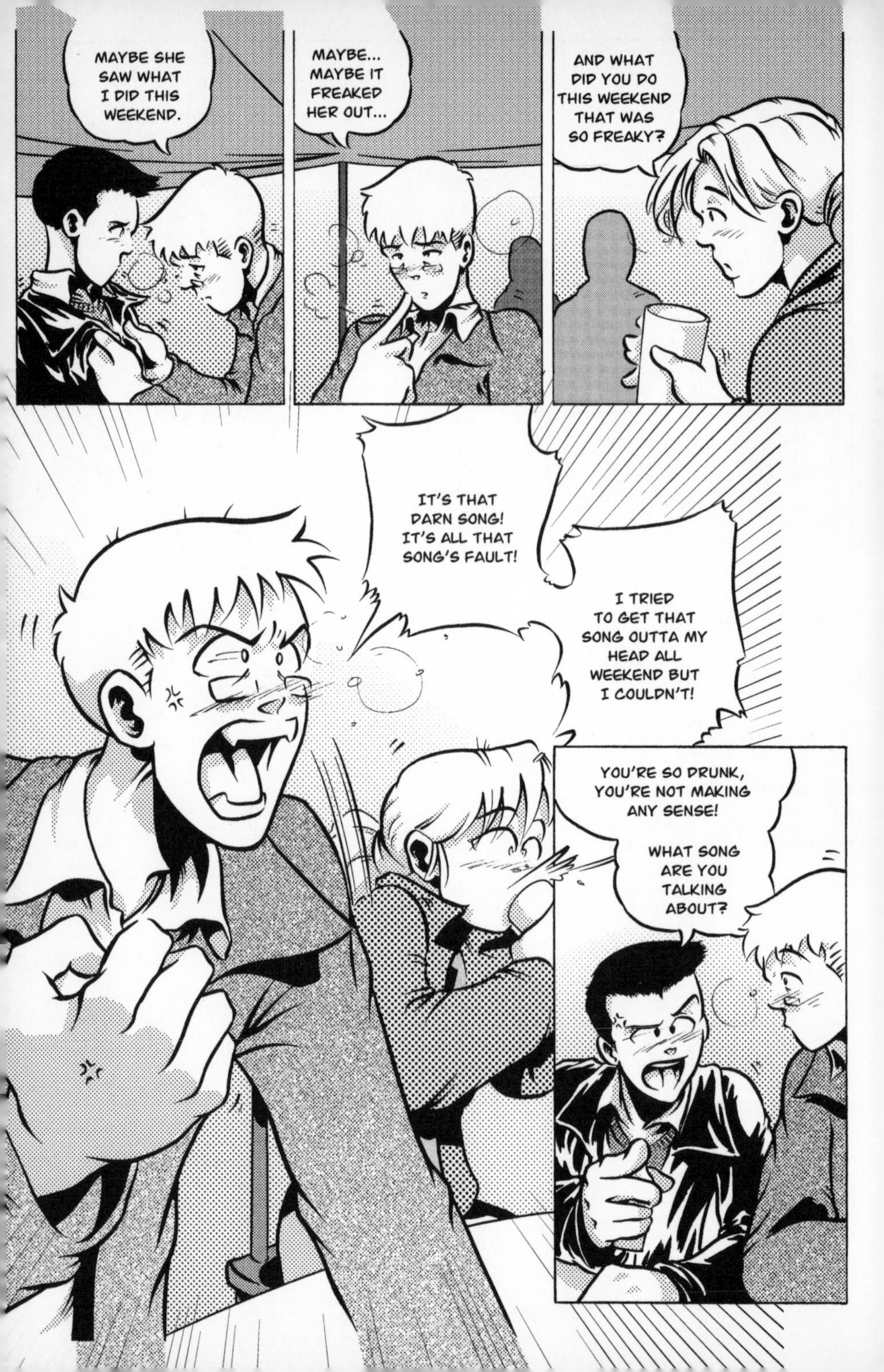
MAYBE SHE SAW WHAT I DID THIS WEEKEND.
MAYBE... MAYBE IT FREAKED HER OUT...
AND WHAT DID YOU DO THIS WEEKEND THAT WAS SO FREAKY?
IT'S THAT DARN SONG! IT'S ALL THAT SONG'S FAULT!
I TRIED TO GET THAT SONG OUTTA MY HEAD ALL WEEKEND BUT I COULDN'T!
YOU'RE SO DRUNK, YOU'RE NOT MAKING ANY SENSE!
WHAT SONG ARE YOU TALKING ABOUT?

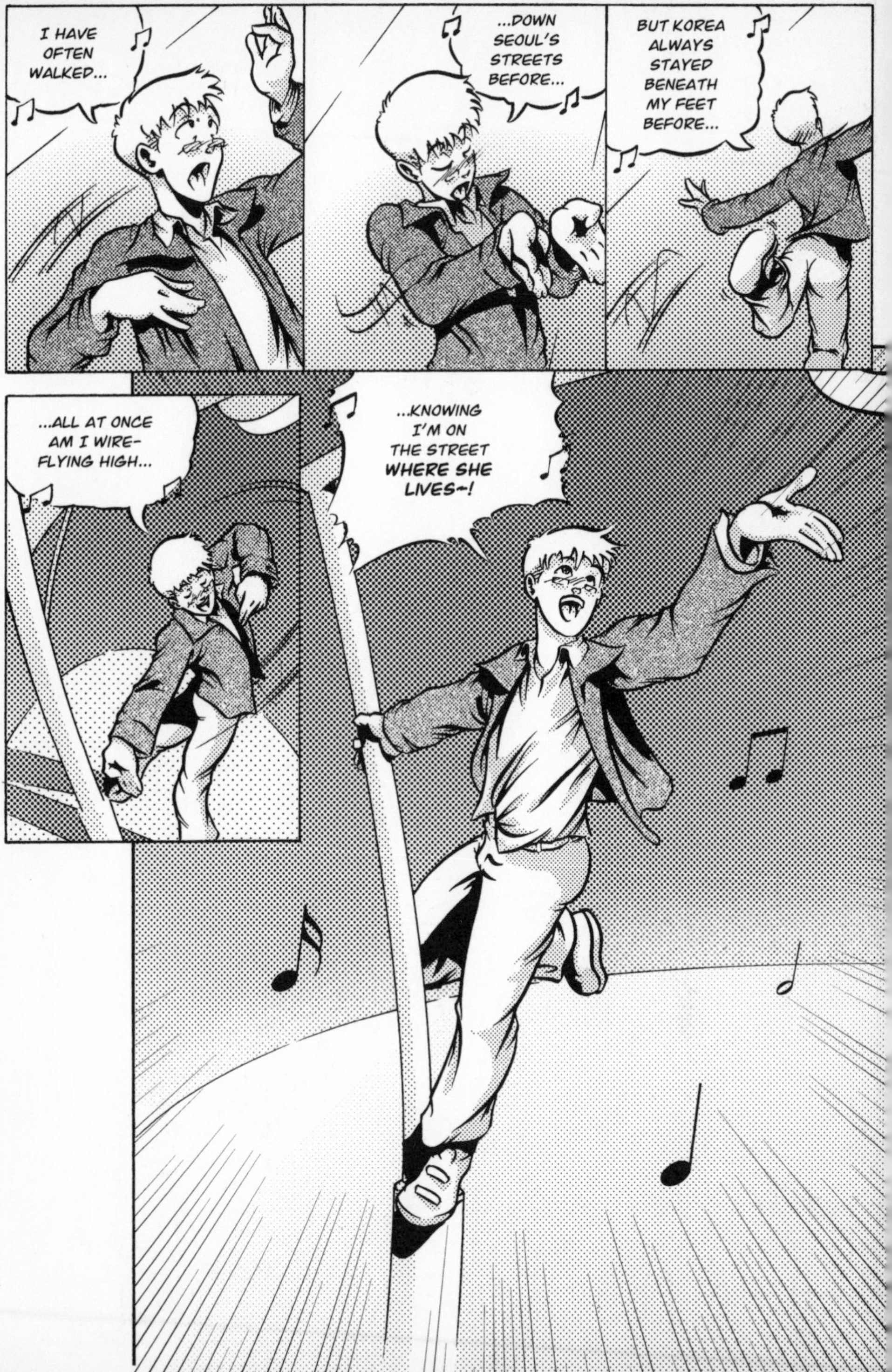
I HAVE OFTEN WALKED...
...DOWN SEOUL'S STREETS BEFORE...
BUT KOREA ALWAYS STAYED BENEATH MY FEET BEFORE...
...ALL AT ONCE AM I WIRE-FLYING HIGH...
...KNOWING I'M ON THE STREET WHERE SHE LIVES~!

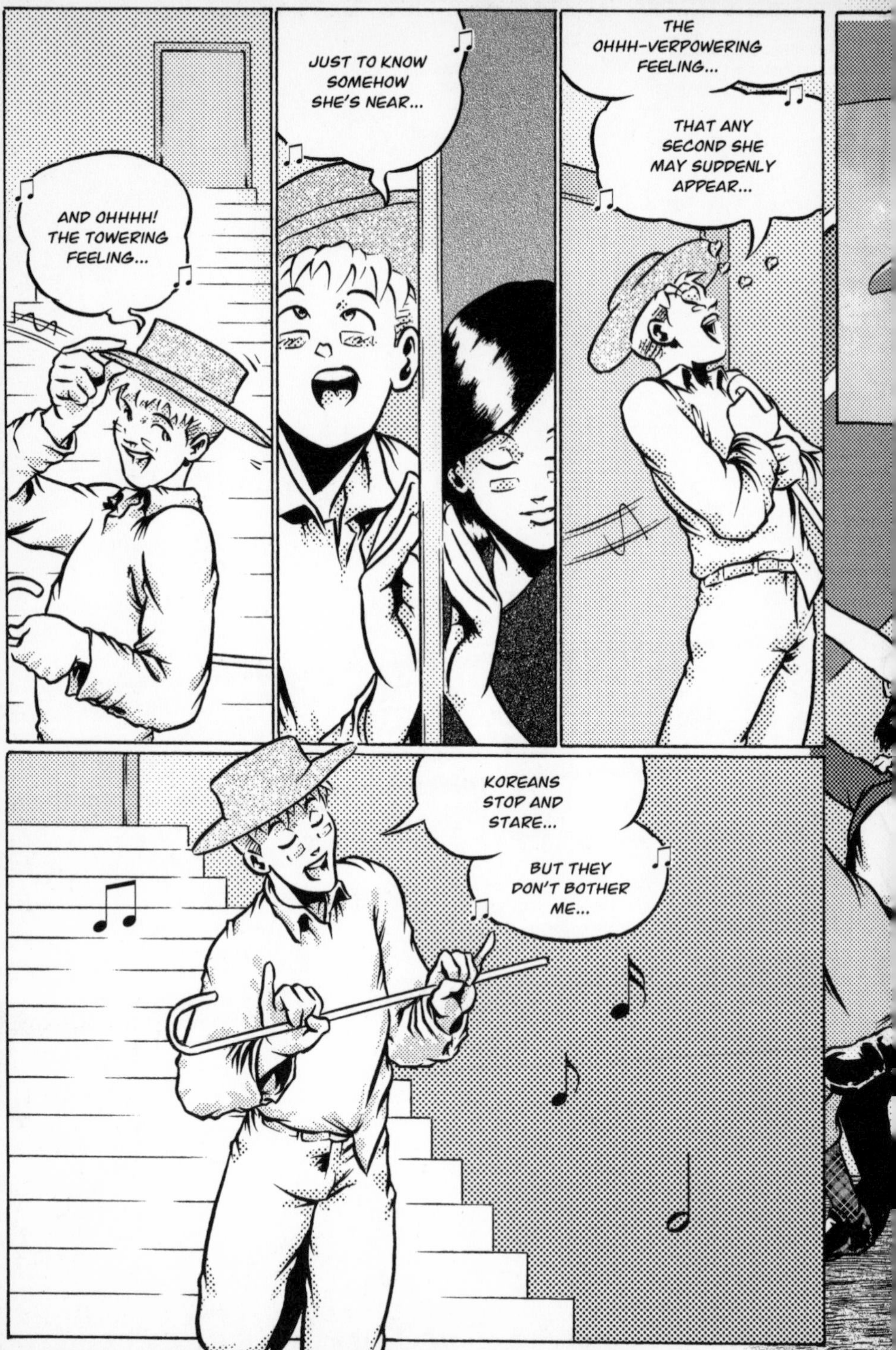
AND OHHHH! THE TOWERING FEELING...
JUST TO KNOW SOMEHOW SHE'S NEAR...
THE OHHH-VERPOWERING FEELING...
THAT ANY SECOND SHE MAY SUDDENLY APPEAR...
KOREANS STOP AND STARE...
BUT THEY DON'T BOTHER ME...

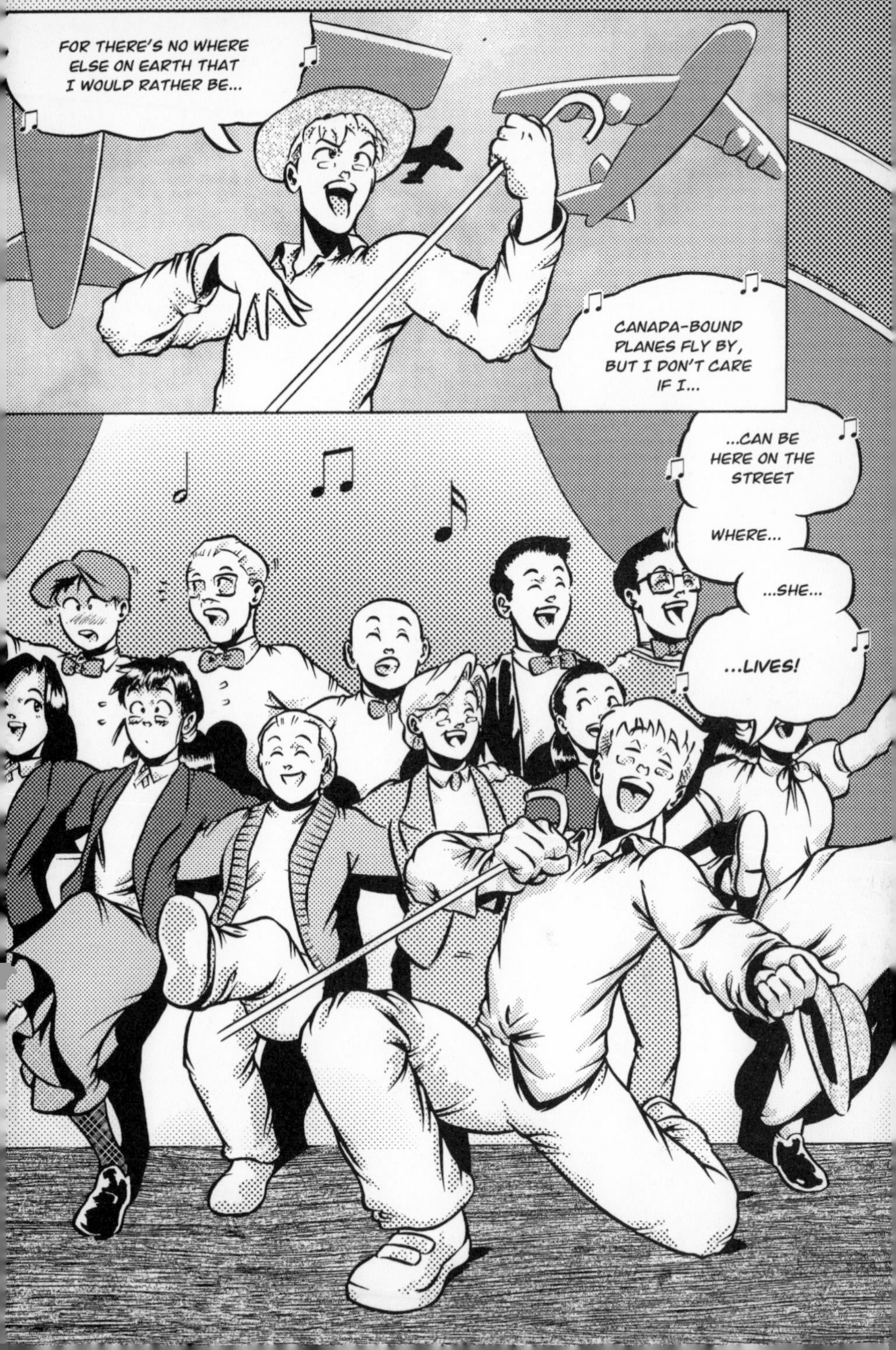
FOR THERE'S NO WHERE ELSE ON EARTH THAT I WOULD RATHER BE...
CANADA-BOUND PLANES FLY BY, BUT I DON'T CARE IF I...
...CAN BE HERE ON THE STREET
WHERE...
...SHE...
...LIVES!

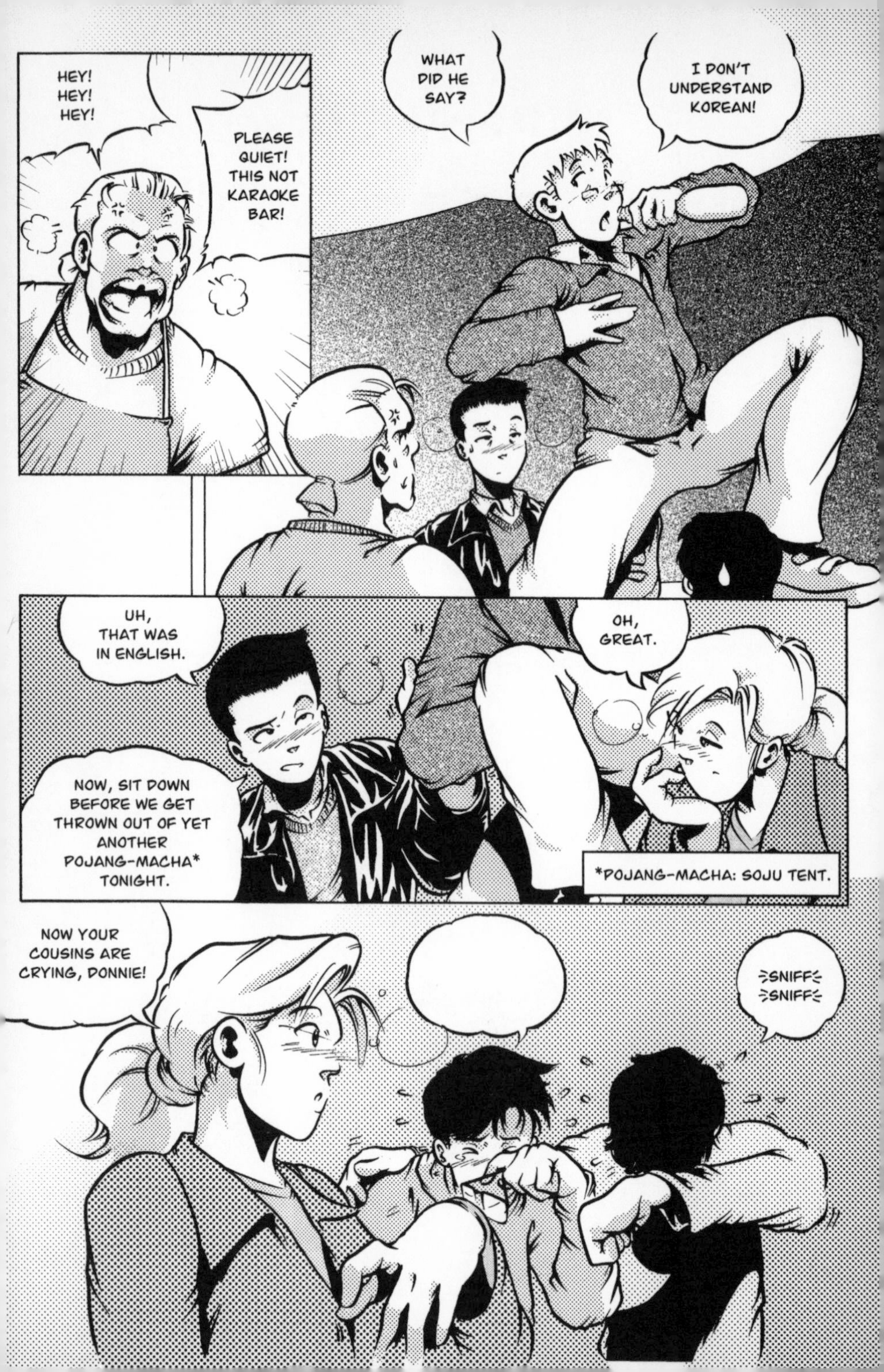
HEY! HEY! HEY!
PLEASE QUIET! THIS NOT KARAOKE BAR!
WHAT DID HE SAY?
I DON'T UNDERSTAND KOREAN!
UH, THAT WAS IN ENGLISH.
OH, GREAT.
NOW, SIT DOWN BEFORE WE GET THROWN OUT OF YET ANOTHER POJANG-MACHA* TONIGHT.
*POJANG-MACHA: SOJU TENT.
NOW YOUR COUSINS ARE CRYING, DONNIE!
SNIFF SNIFF

Chapter 16

HANA BODY HOME?

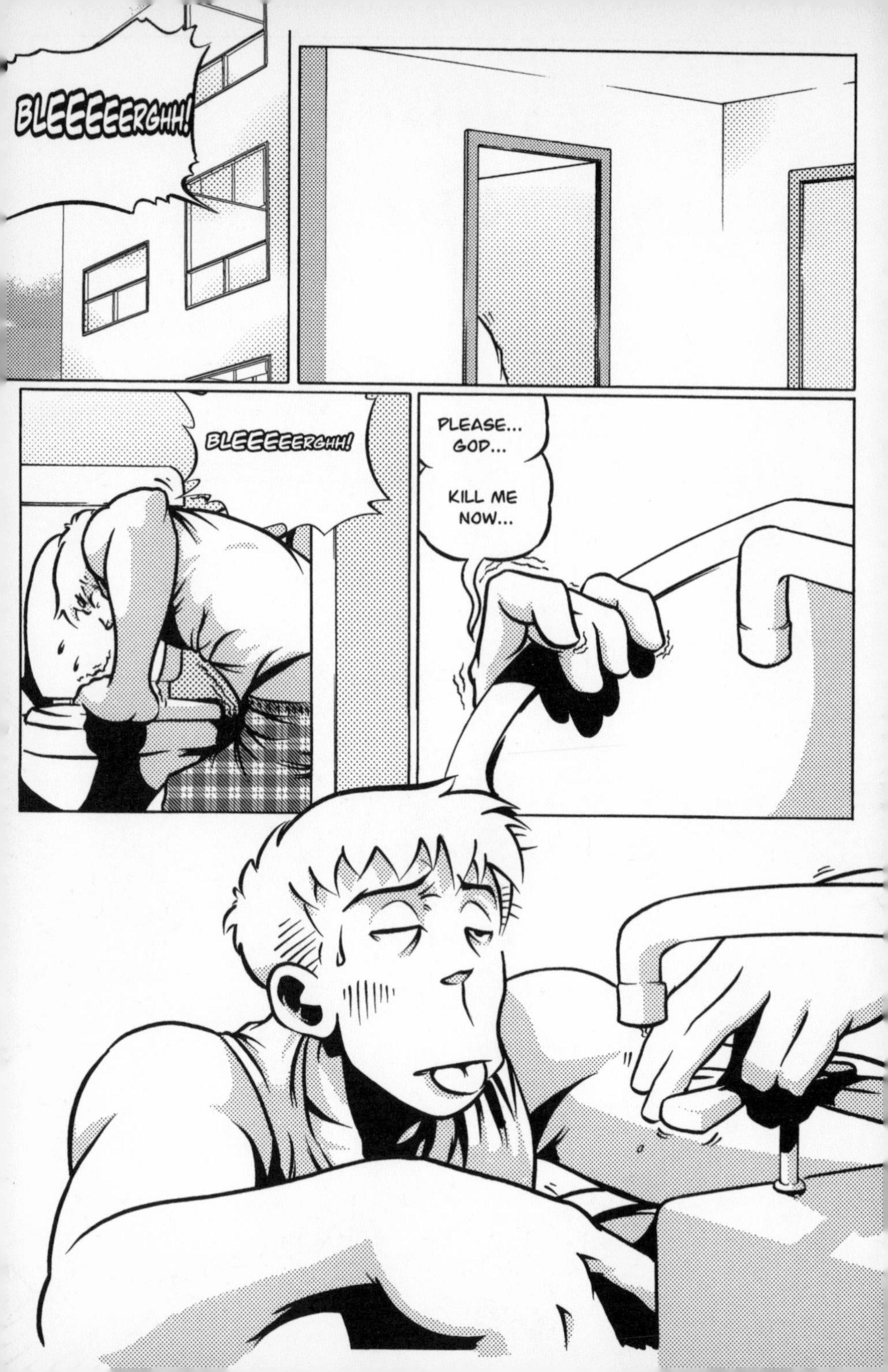
BLEEEEERGHH!
BLEEEEERGHH!
PLEASE... GOD...
KILL ME NOW...

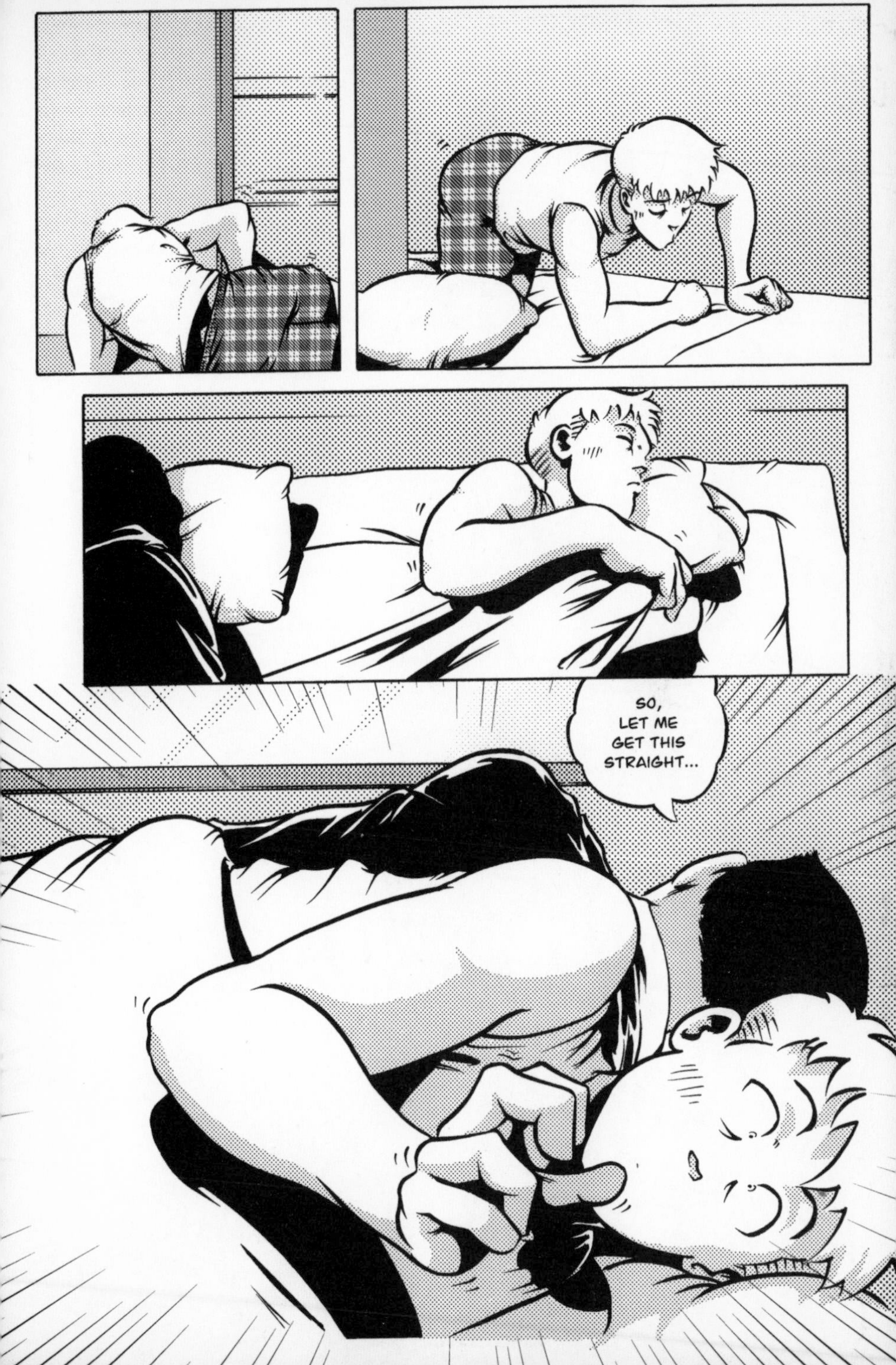
SO, LET ME GET THIS STRAIGHT...

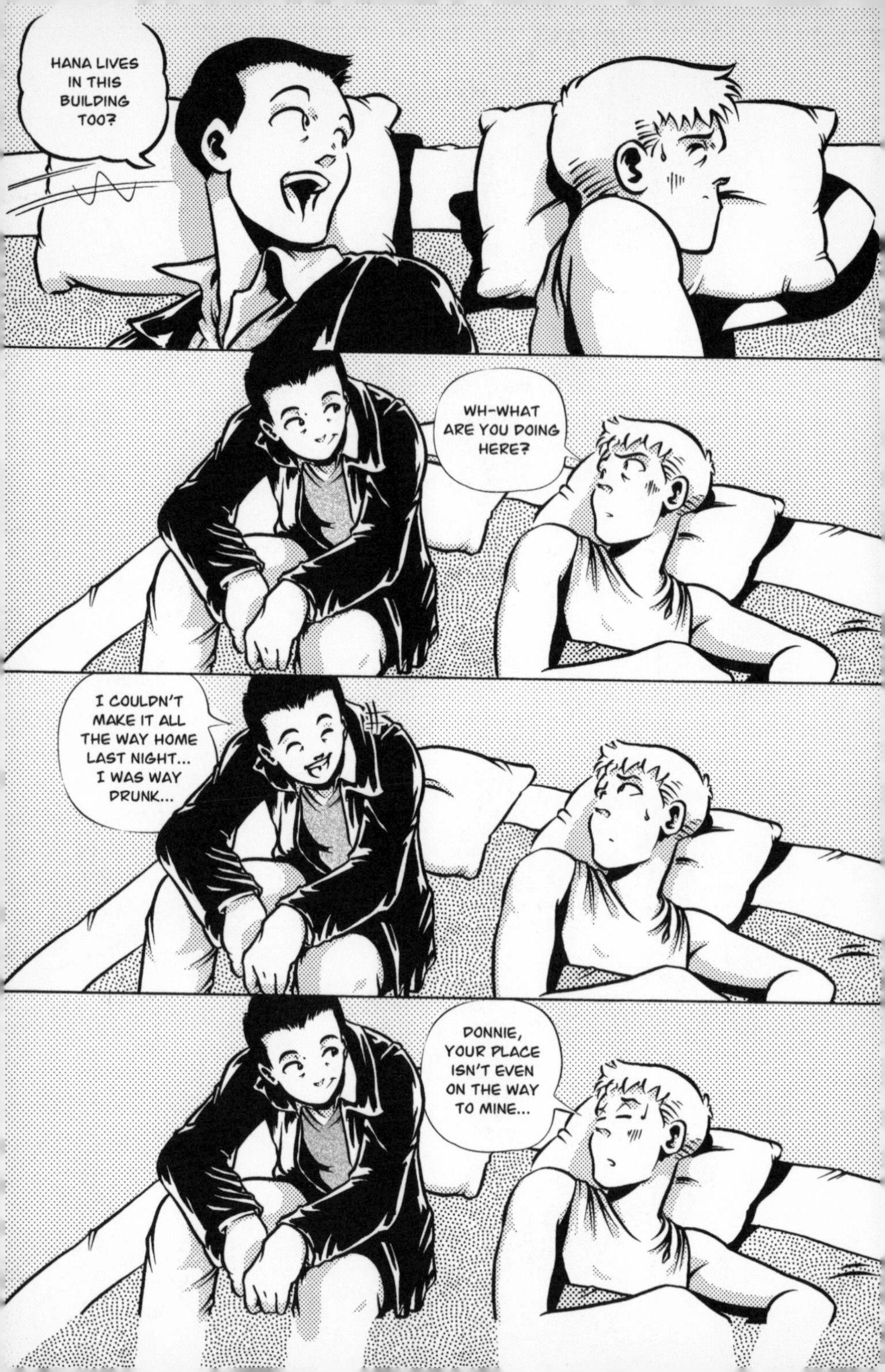
HANA LIVES IN THIS BUILDING TOO?
WH-WHAT ARE YOU DOING HERE?
I COULDN'T MAKE IT ALL THE WAY HOME LAST NIGHT... I WAS WAY DRUNK...
DONNIE, YOUR PLACE ISN'T EVEN ON THE WAY TO MINE...

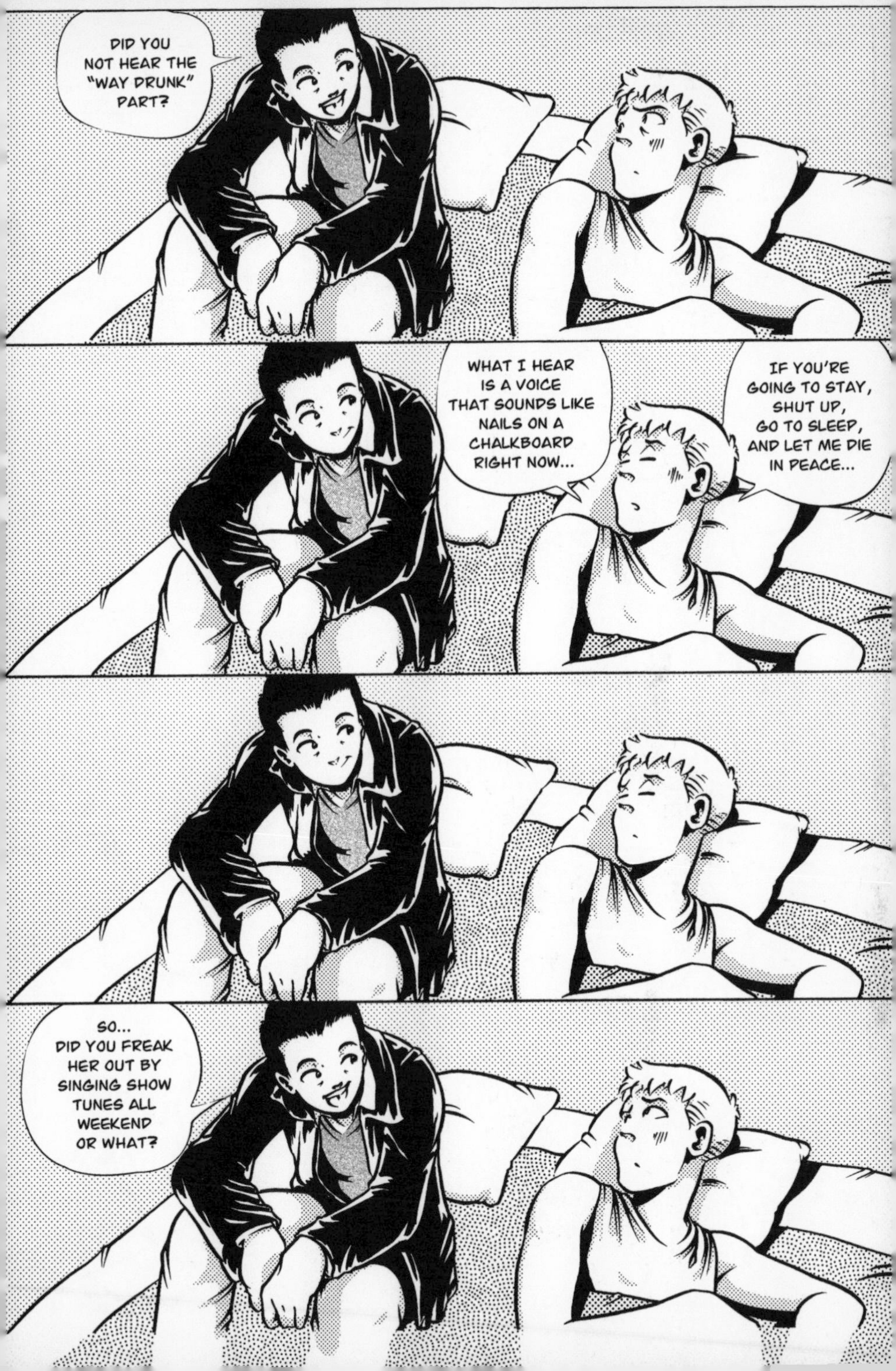
DID YOU NOT HEAR THE "WAY DRUNK" PART?
WHAT I HEAR IS A VOICE THAT SOUNDS LIKE NAILS ON A CHALKBOARD RIGHT NOW...
IF YOU'RE GOING TO STAY, SHUT UP, GO TO SLEEP, AND LET ME DIE IN PEACE...
SO... DID YOU FREAK HER OUT BY SINGING SHOW TUNES ALL WEEKEND OR WHAT?

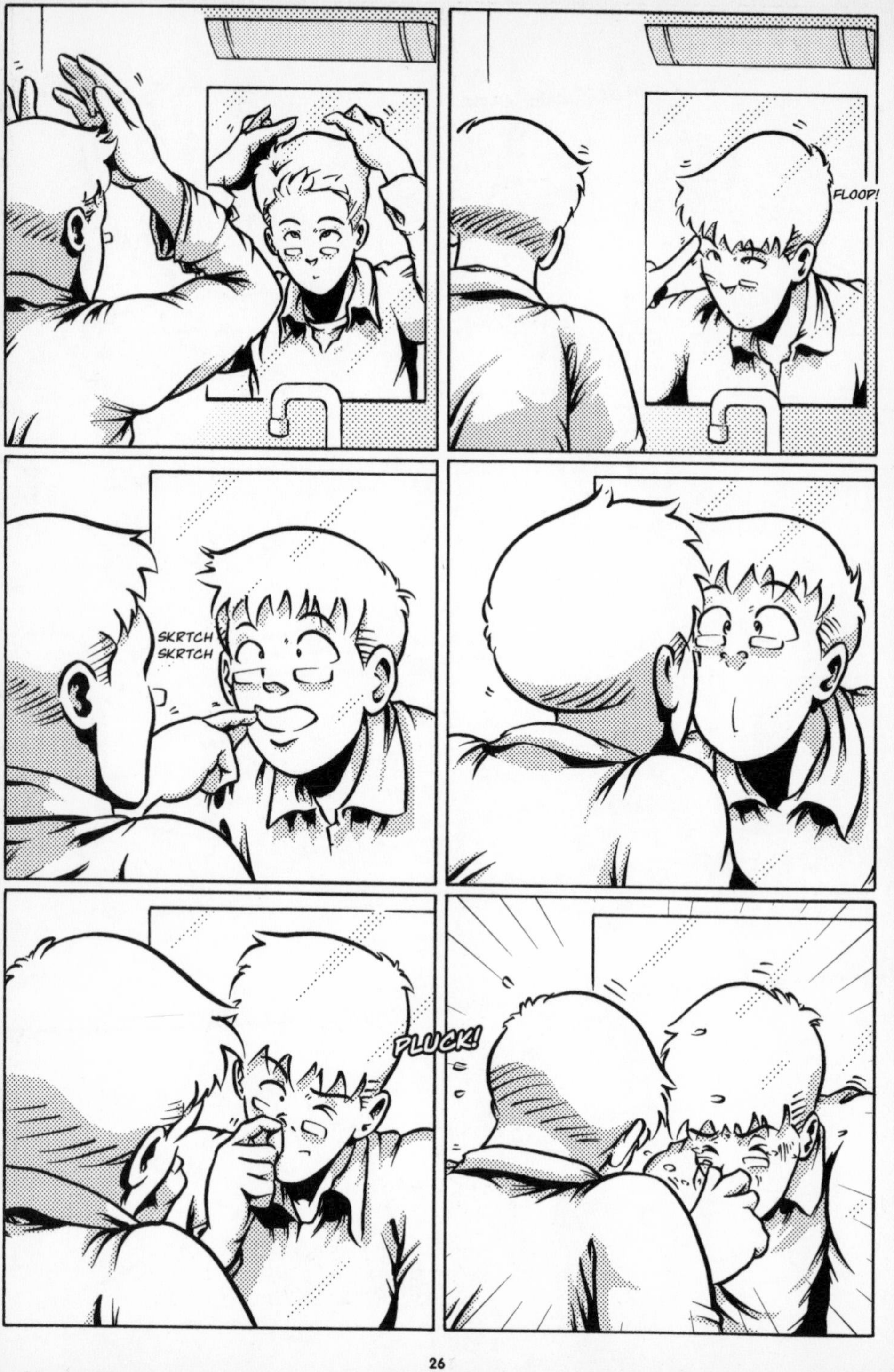
FLOOP!
SKRTCH
SKRTCH
PLUCK!

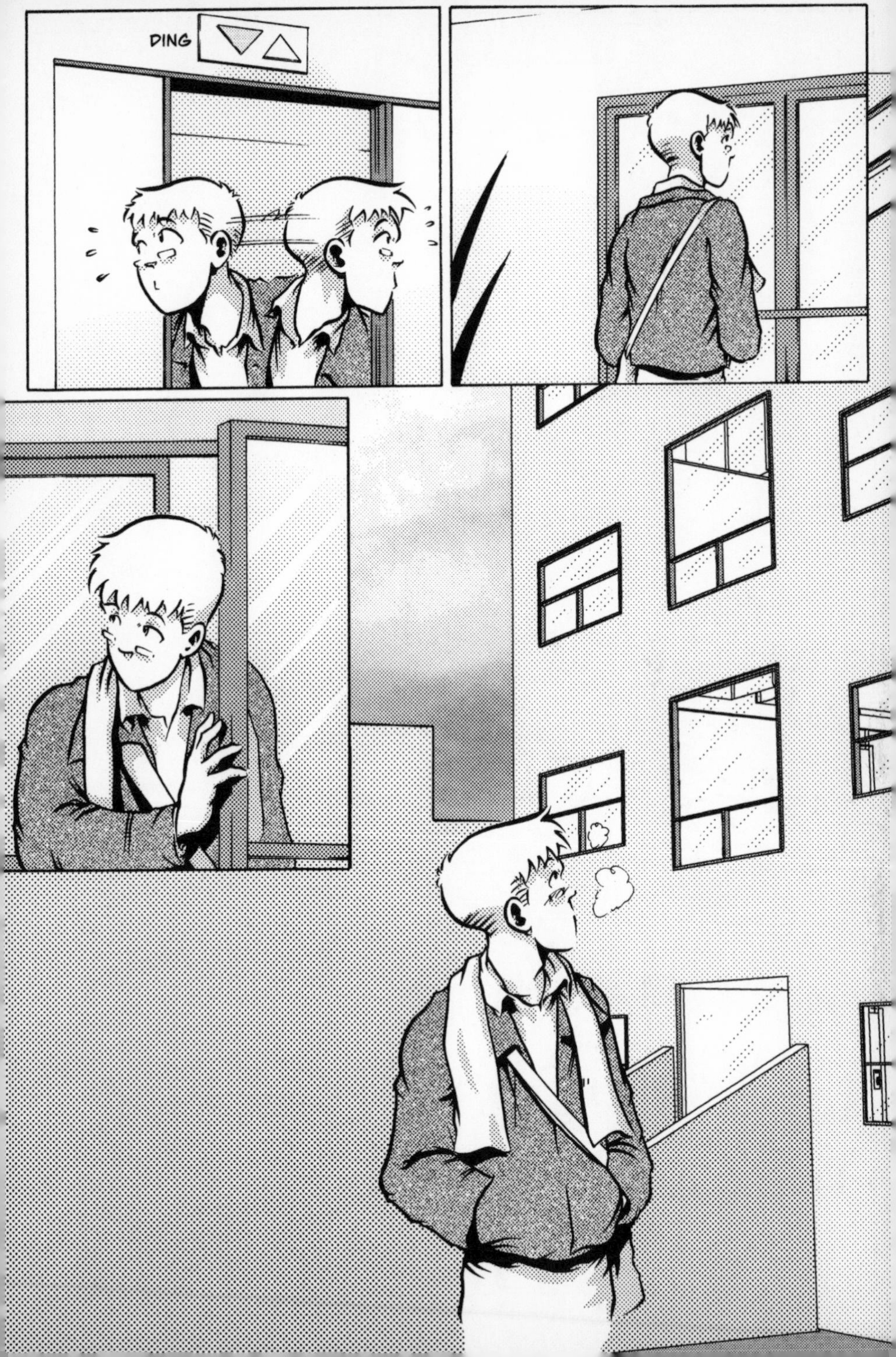
DING

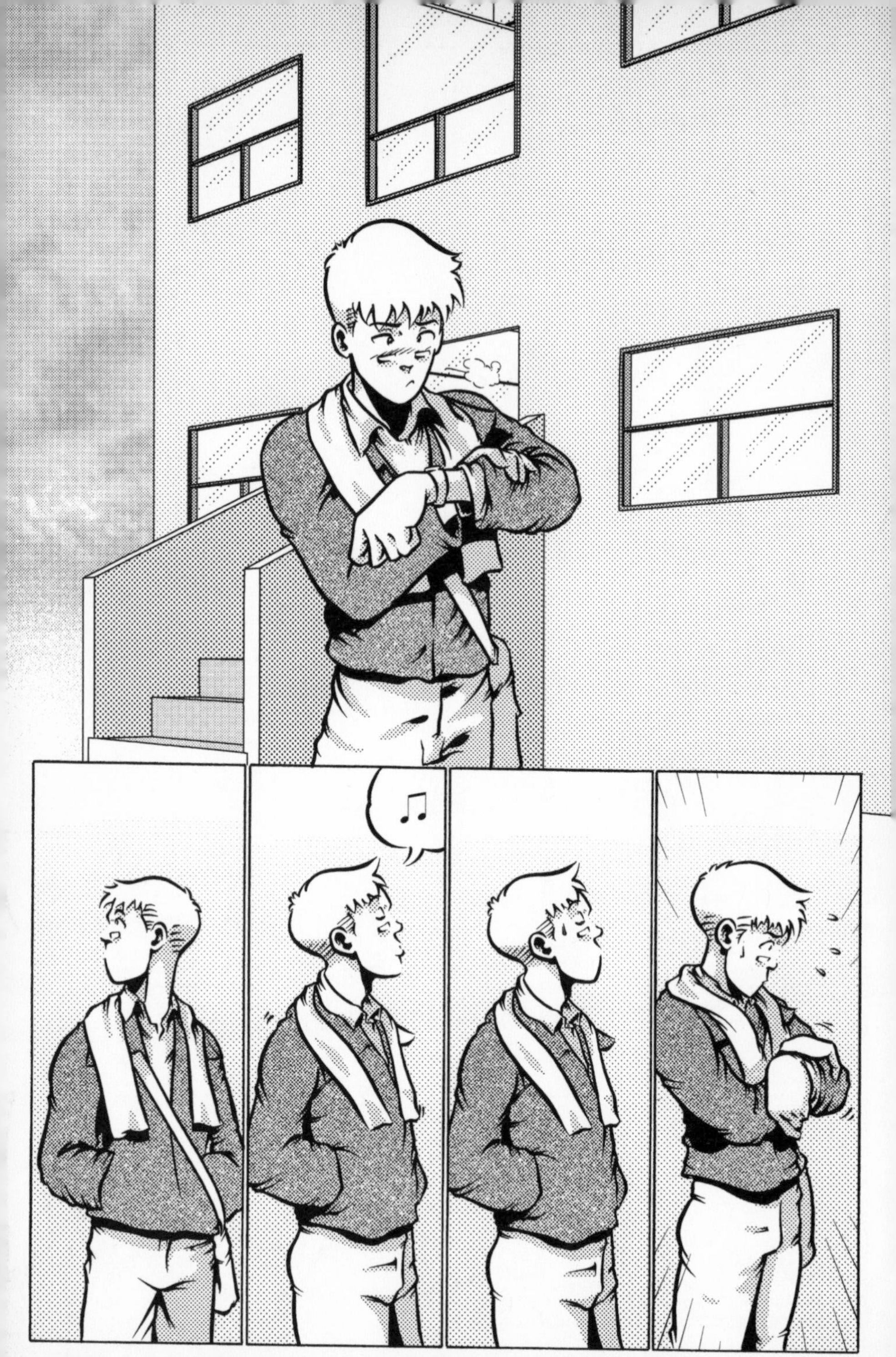

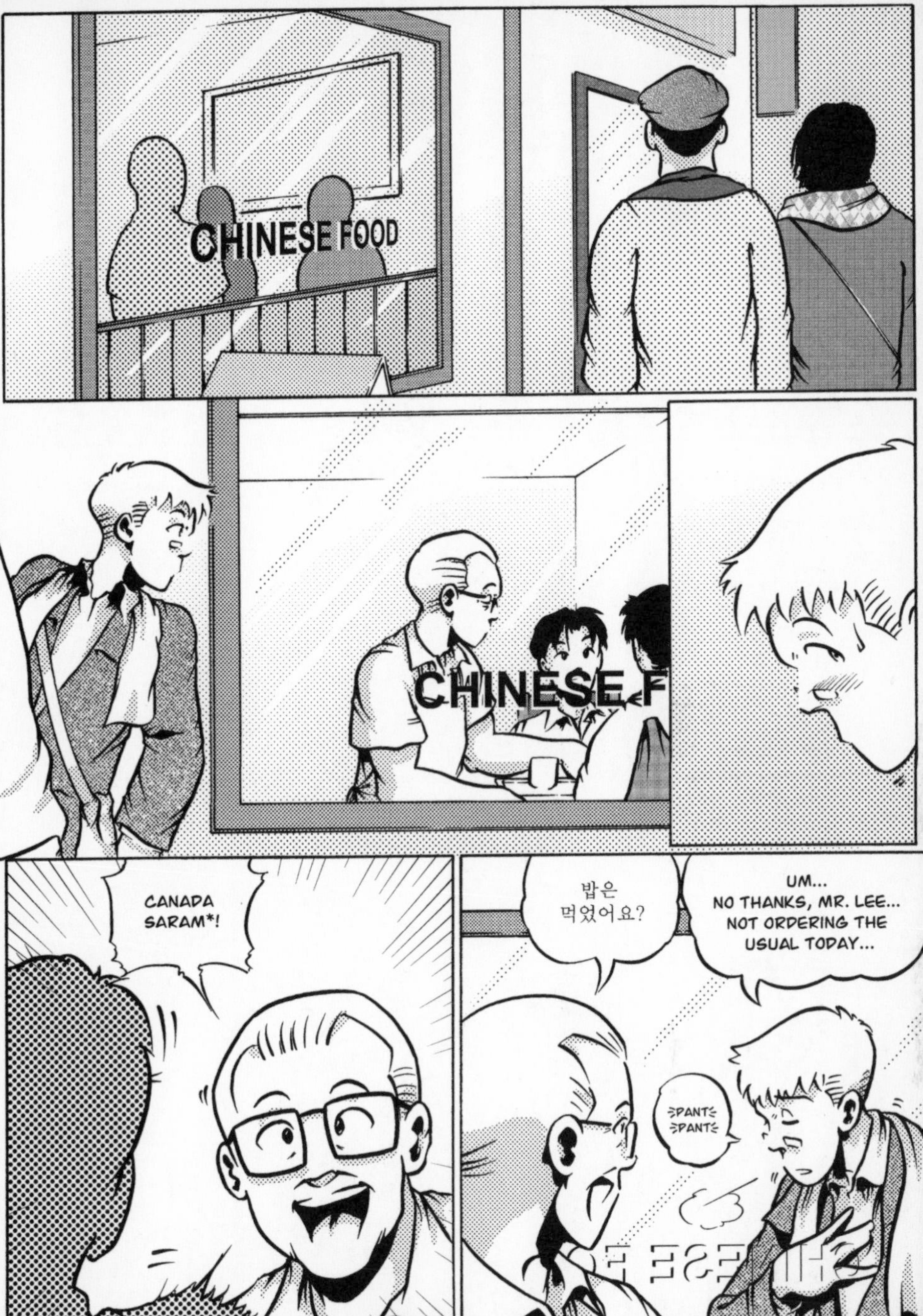
CHINESE FOOD
CHINESE F
CANADA SARAM*!
*SARAM: PERSON
밥은 먹었어요?
UM... NO THANKS, MR. LEE... NOT ORDERING THE USUAL TODAY...
PANT PANT

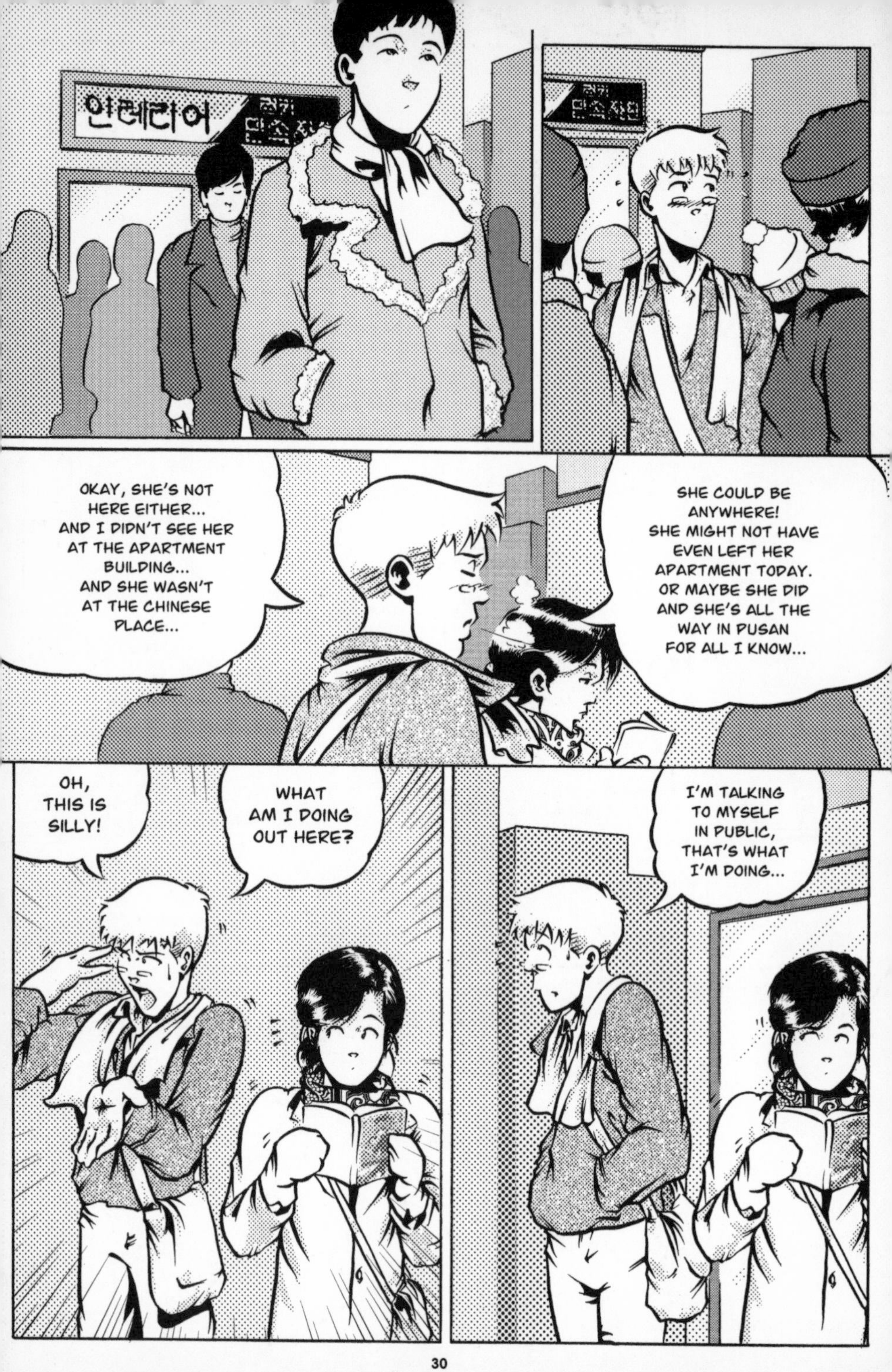
OKAY, SHE'S NOT HERE EITHER... AND I DIDN'T SEE HER AT THE APARTMENT BUILDING... AND SHE WASN'T AT THE CHINESE PLACE...
SHE COULD BE ANYWHERE! SHE MIGHT NOT HAVE EVEN LEFT HER APARTMENT TODAY. OR MAYBE SHE DID AND SHE'S ALL THE WAY IN PUSAN FOR ALL I KNOW...
OH, THIS IS SILLY!
WHAT AM I DOING OUT HERE?
I'M TALKING TO MYSELF IN PUBLIC, THAT'S WHAT I'M DOING...

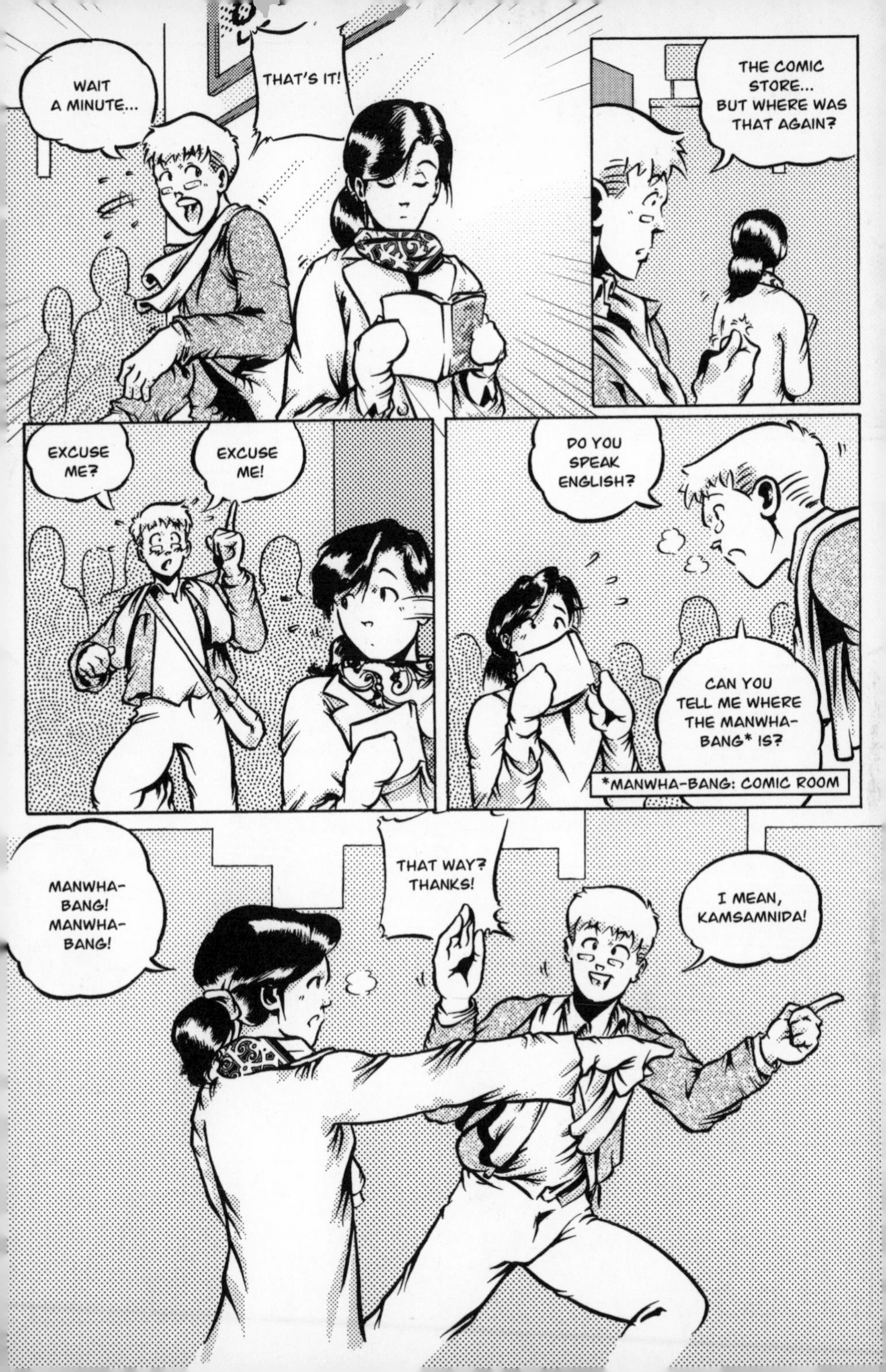
WAIT A MINUTE...
THAT'S IT!
THE COMIC STORE... BUT WHERE WAS THAT AGAIN?
EXCUSE ME?
EXCUSE ME!
DO YOU SPEAK ENGLISH?
CAN YOU TELL ME WHERE THE MANWHA-BANG* IS?
*MANWHA-BANG: COMIC ROOM
MANWHA-BANG! MANWHA-BANG!
THAT WAY? THANKS!
I MEAN, KAMSAMNIDA!

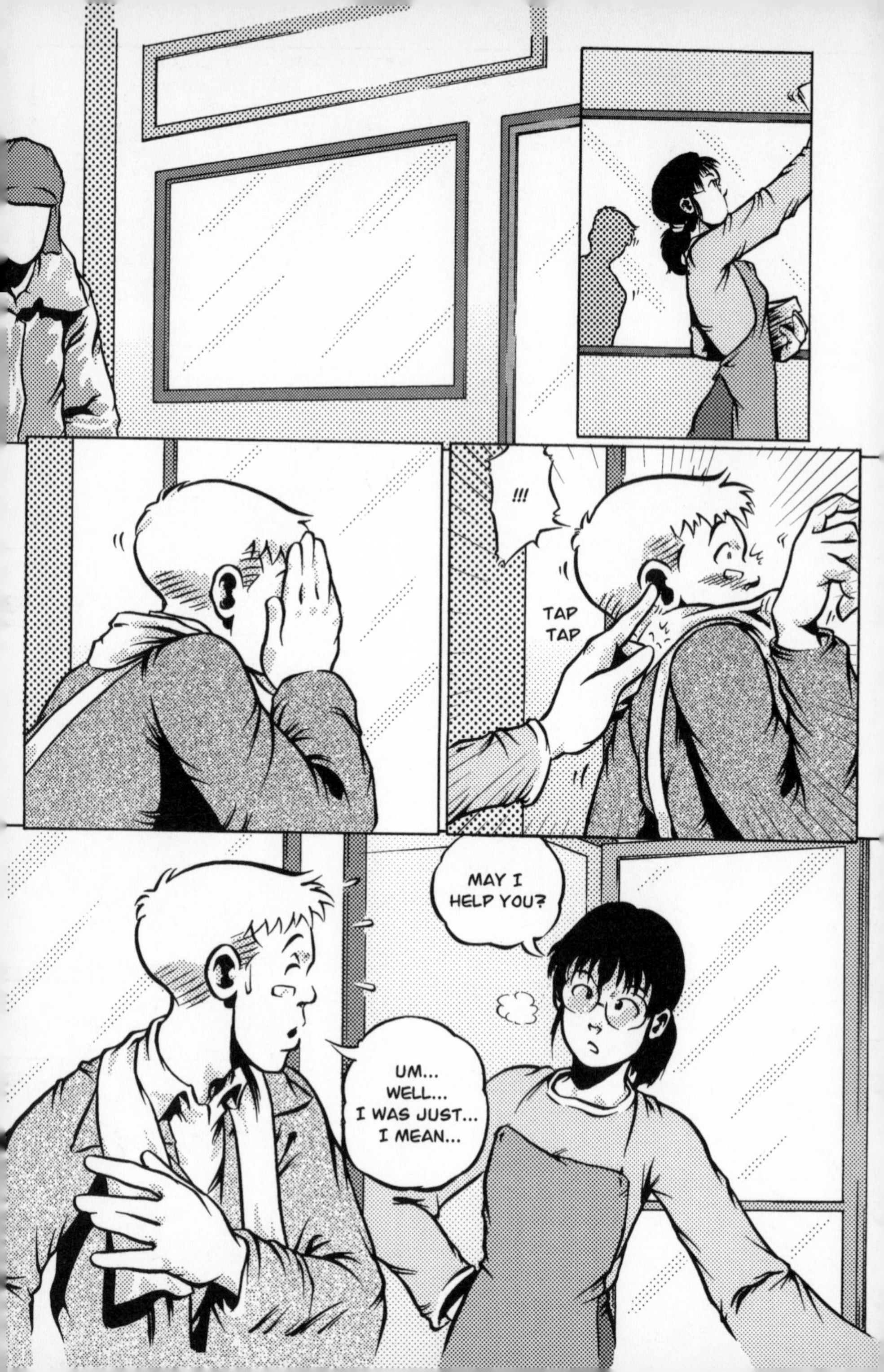
!!!
TAP
TAP
MAY I HELP YOU?
UM... WELL... I WAS JUST... I MEAN...

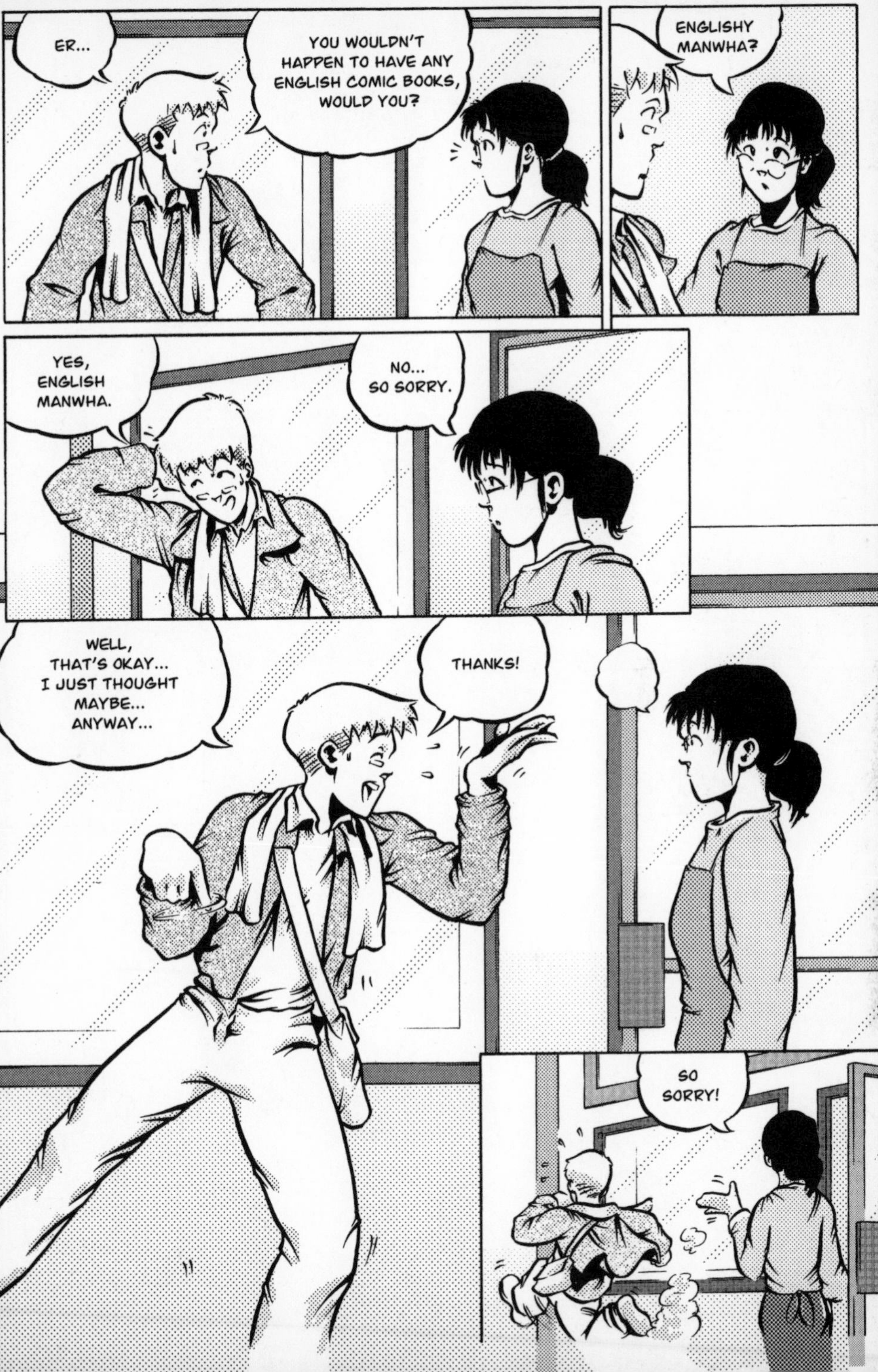
ER...
YOU WOULDN'T HAPPEN TO HAVE ANY ENGLISH COMIC BOOKS, WOULD YOU?
ENGLISHY MANWHA?
YES, ENGLISH MANWHA.
NO... SO SORRY.
WELL, THAT'S OKAY... I JUST THOUGHT MAYBE... ANYWAY...
THANKS!
SO SORRY!

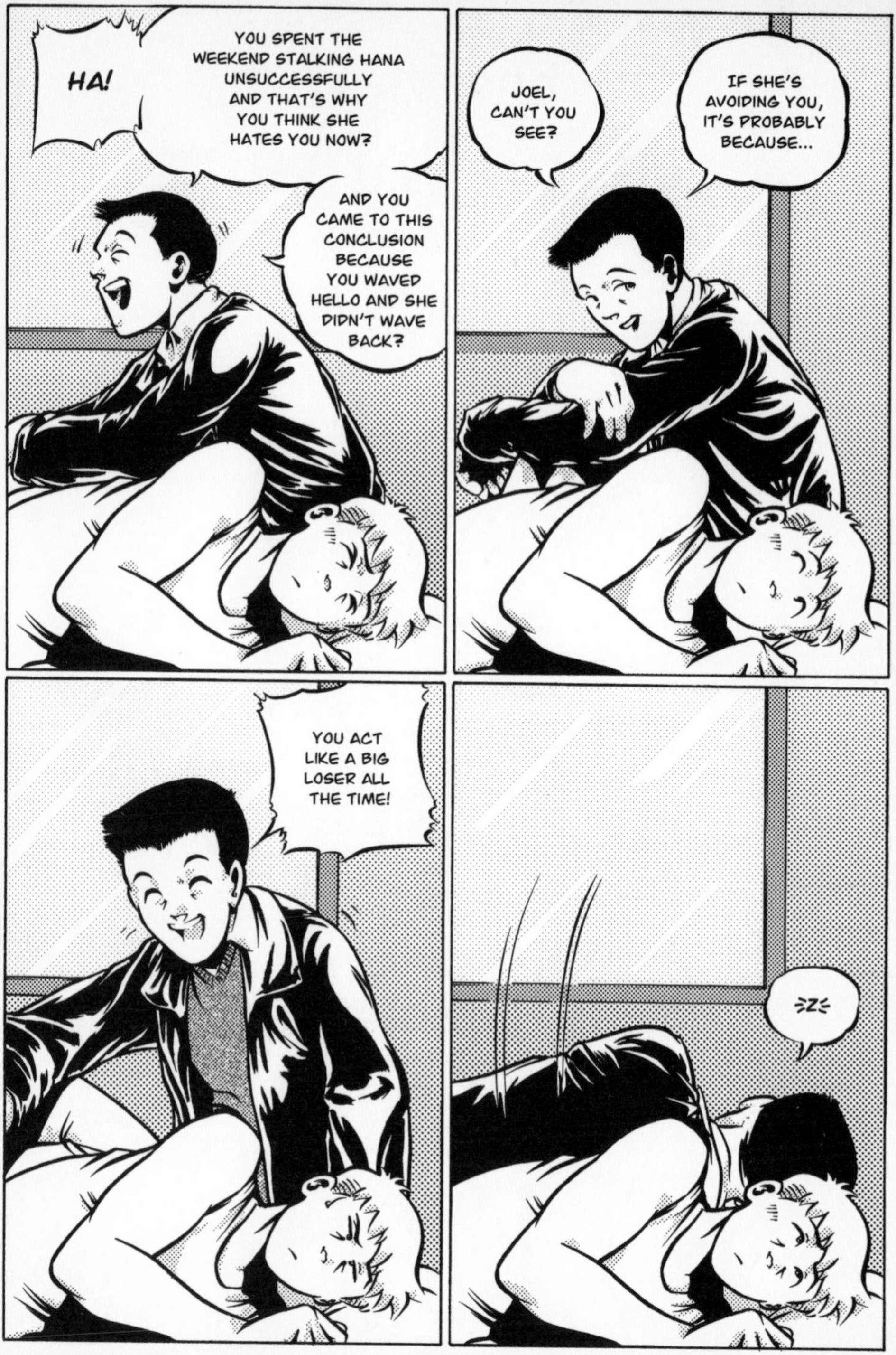
HA!
YOU SPENT THE WEEKEND STALKING HANA UNSUCCESSFULLY AND THAT'S WHY YOU THINK SHE HATES YOU NOW?
AND YOU CAME TO THIS CONCLUSION BECAUSE YOU WAVED HELLO AND SHE DIDN'T WAVE BACK?
JOEL, CAN'T YOU SEE?
IF SHE'S AVOIDING YOU, IT'S PROBABLY BECAUSE...
YOU ACT LIKE A BIG LOSER ALL THE TIME!
Z

Chapter 17

HIGH NUUN

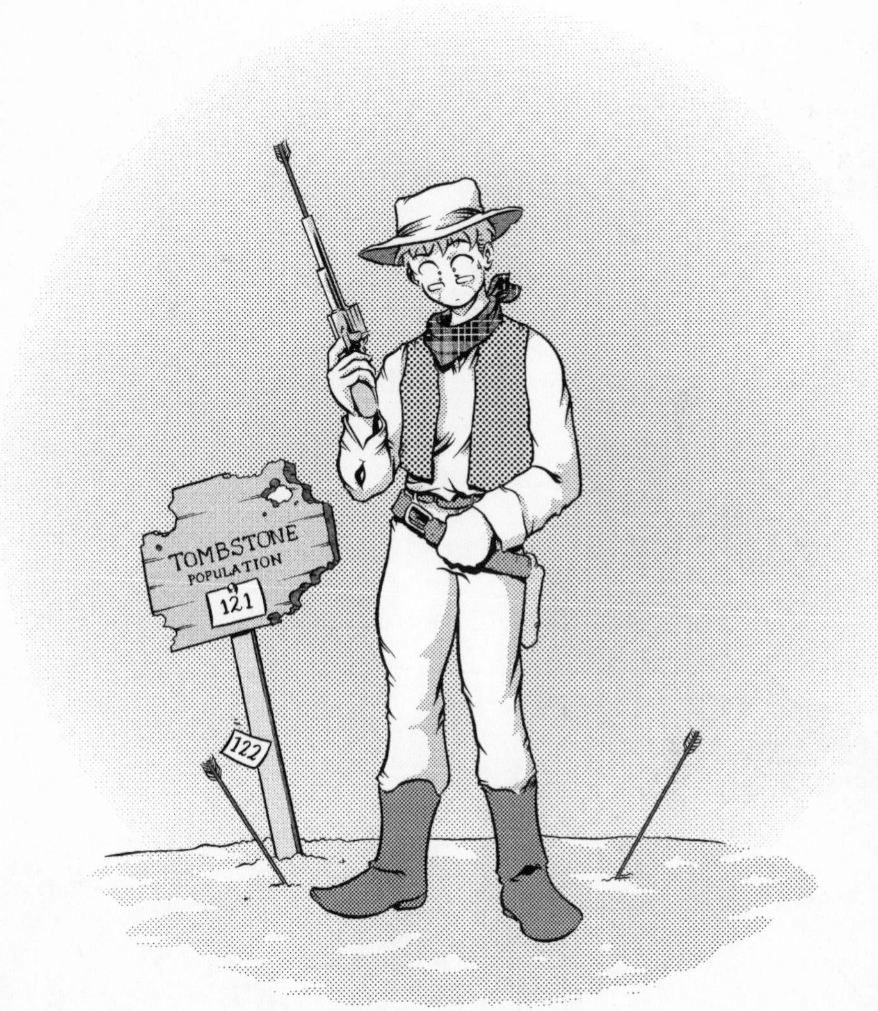

TOMBSTONE
POPULATION
121
122

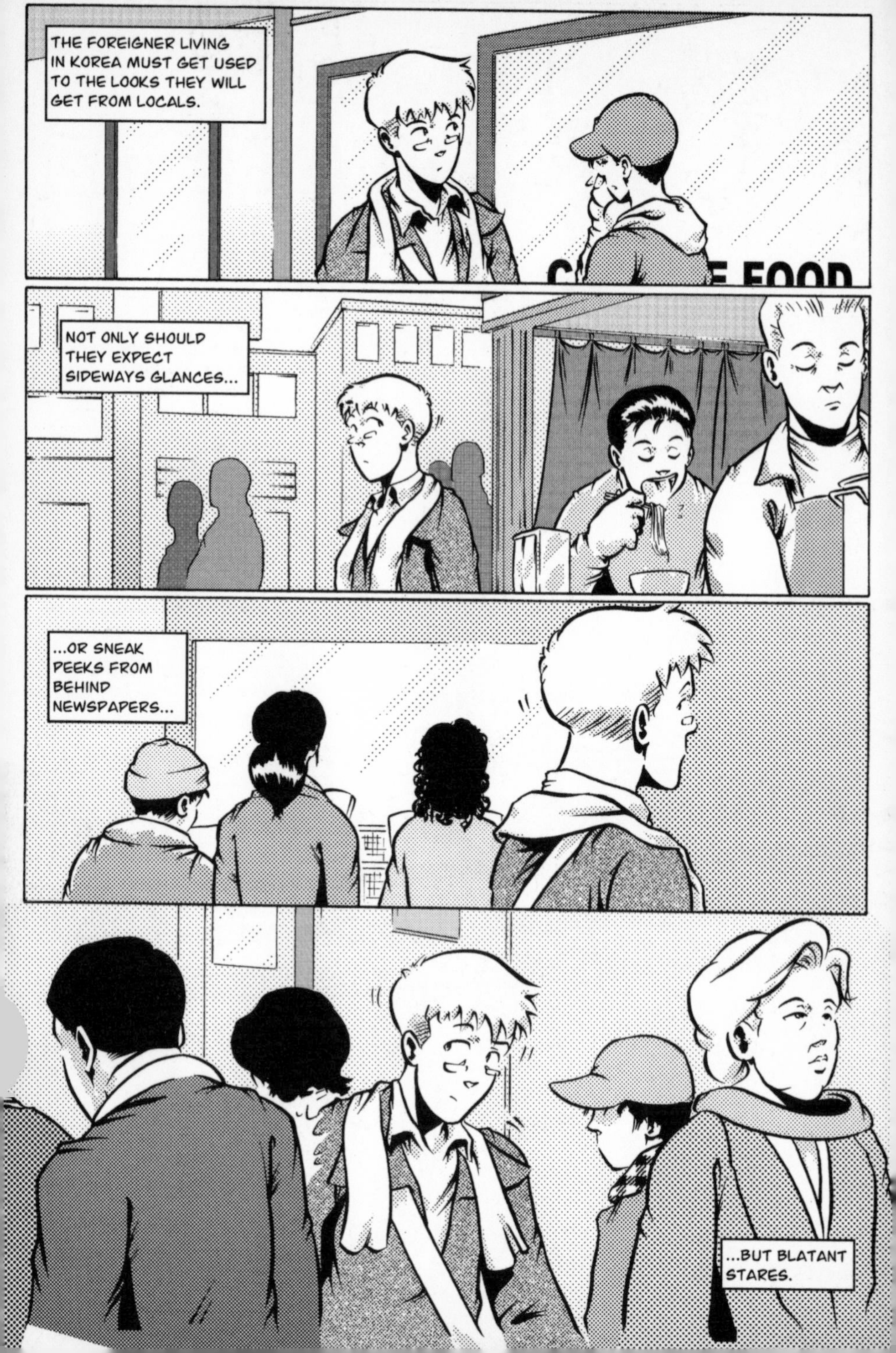
THE FOREIGNER LIVING IN KOREA MUST GET USED TO THE LOOKS THEY WILL GET FROM LOCALS.
NOT ONLY SHOULD THEY EXPECT SIDEWAYS GLANCES...
...OR SNEAK PEEKS FROM BEHIND NEWSPAPERS...
...BUT BLATANT STARES.

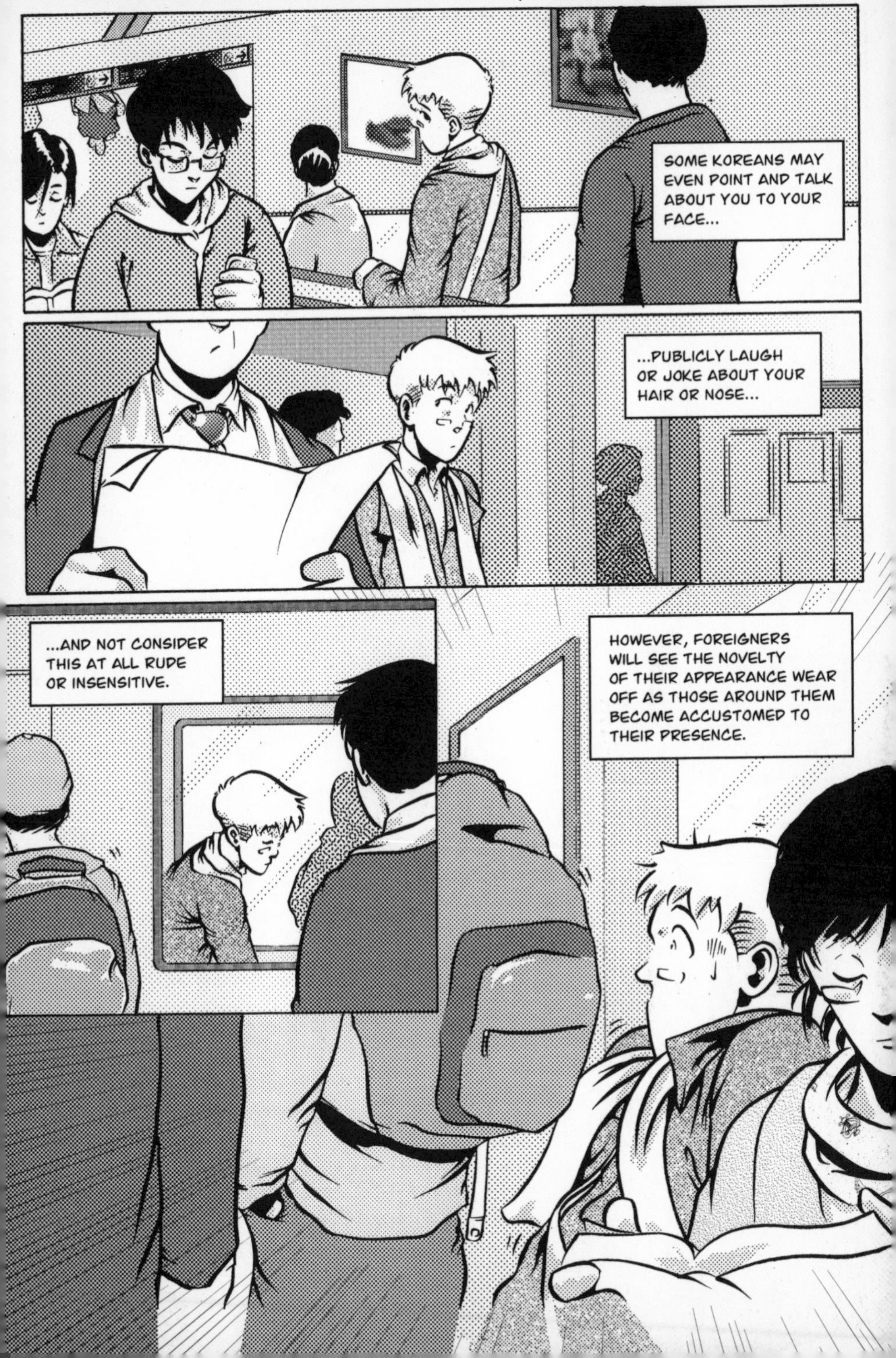
SOME KOREANS MAY EVEN POINT AND TALK ABOUT YOU TO YOUR FACE...
...PUBLICLY LAUGH OR JOKE ABOUT YOUR HAIR OR NOSE...
...AND NOT CONSIDER THIS AT ALL RUDE OR INSENSITIVE.
HOWEVER, FOREIGNERS WILL SEE THE NOVELTY OF THEIR APPEARANCE WEAR OFF AS THOSE AROUND THEM BECOME ACCUSTOMED TO THEIR PRESENCE.

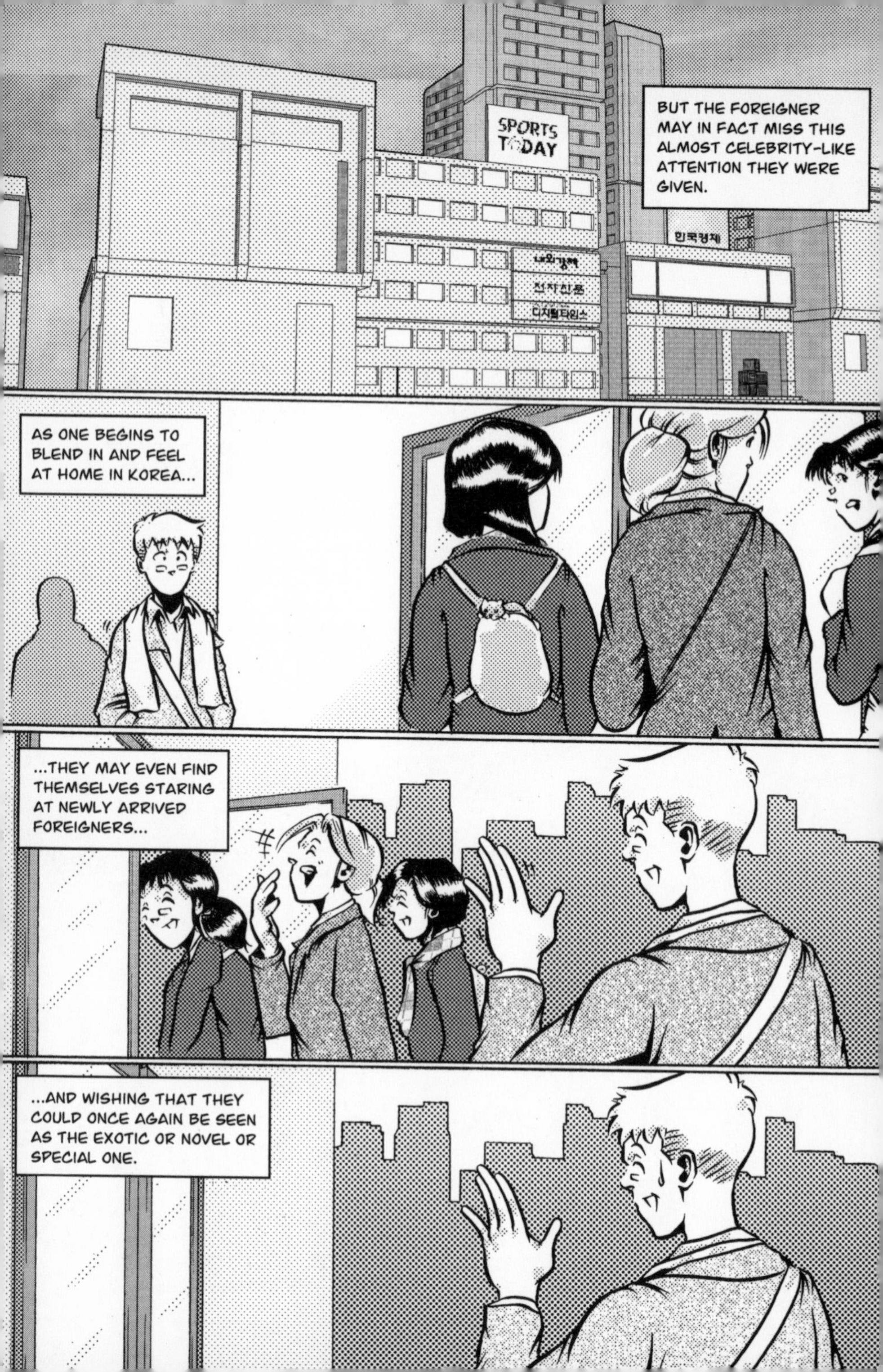
SPORTS TODAY
BUT THE FOREIGNER MAY IN FACT MISS THIS ALMOST CELEBRITY-LIKE ATTENTION THEY WERE GIVEN.
내외경제
전자신문
디지털타임스
한국경제
AS ONE BEGINS TO BLEND IN AND FEEL AT HOME IN KOREA...
...THEY MAY EVEN FIND THEMSELVES STARING AT NEWLY ARRIVED FOREIGNERS...
...AND WISHING THAT THEY COULD ONCE AGAIN BE SEEN AS THE EXOTIC OR NOVEL OR SPECIAL ONE.

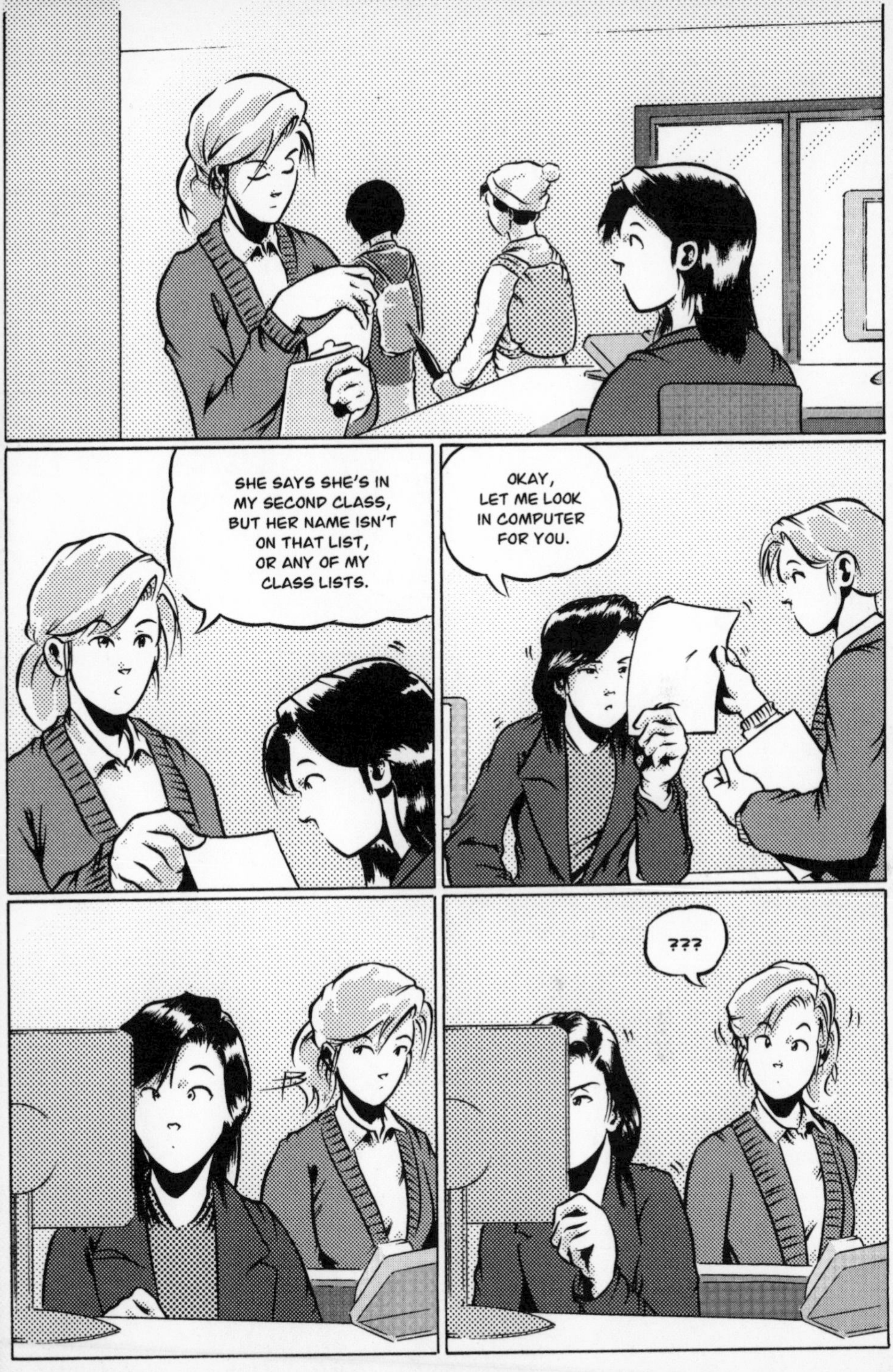
SHE SAYS SHE'S IN MY SECOND CLASS, BUT HER NAME ISN'T ON THAT LIST, OR ANY OF MY CLASS LISTS.
OKAY, LET ME LOOK IN COMPUTER FOR YOU.
???

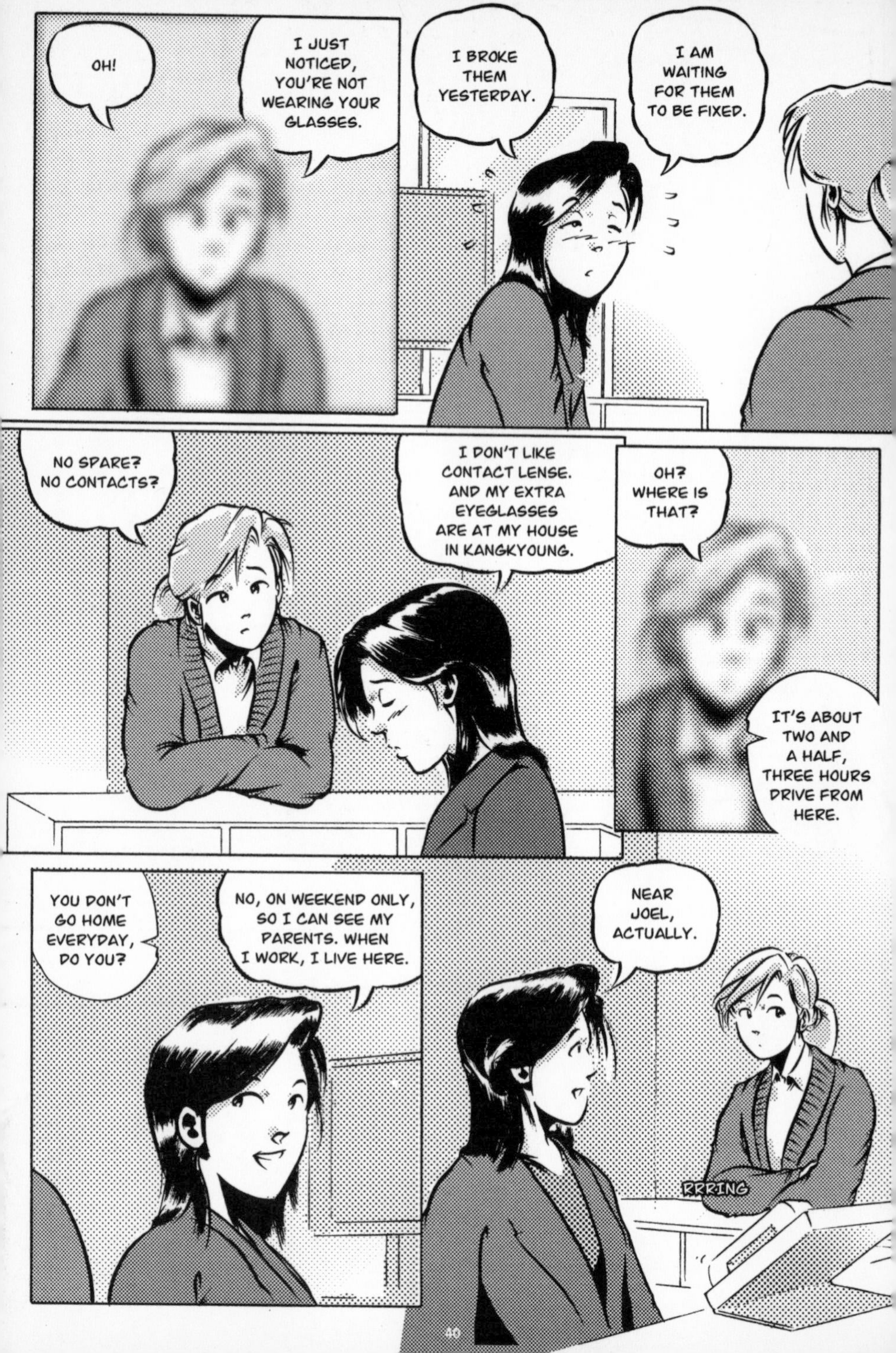
OH!
I JUST NOTICED, YOU'RE NOT WEARING YOUR GLASSES.
I BROKE THEM YESTERDAY.
I AM WAITING FOR THEM TO BE FIXED.
NO SPARE? NO CONTACTS?
I DON'T LIKE CONTACT LENSE. AND MY EXTRA EYEGLASSES ARE AT MY HOUSE IN KANGKYOUNG.
OH? WHERE IS THAT?
IT'S ABOUT TWO AND A HALF, THREE HOURS DRIVE FROM HERE.
YOU DON'T GO HOME EVERYDAY, DO YOU?
NO, ON WEEKEND ONLY, SO I CAN SEE MY PARENTS. WHEN I WORK, I LIVE HERE.
NEAR JOEL, ACTUALLY.
RRRING

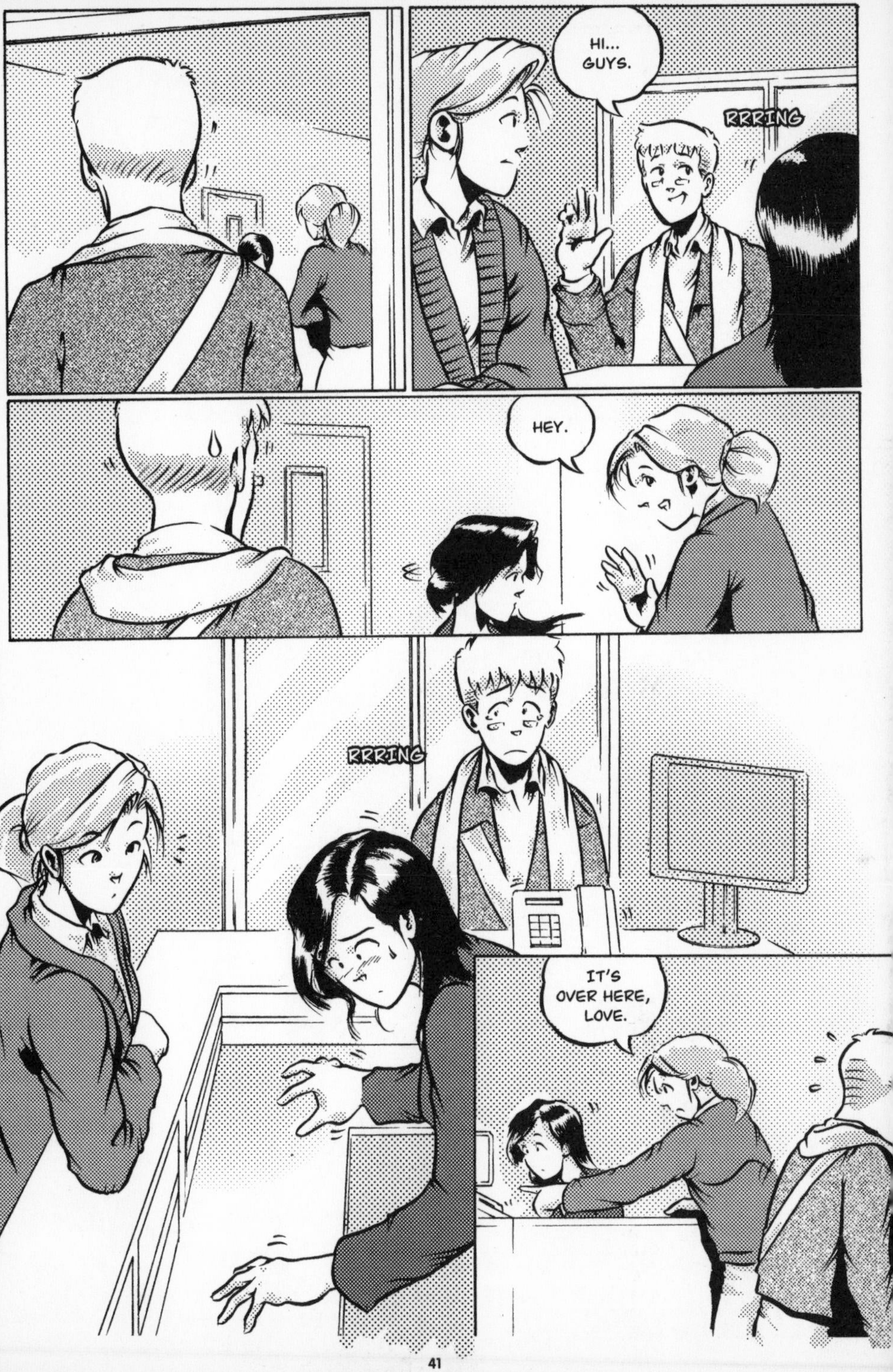
HI... GUYS.
RRRING
HEY.
RRRING
IT'S OVER HERE, LOVE.

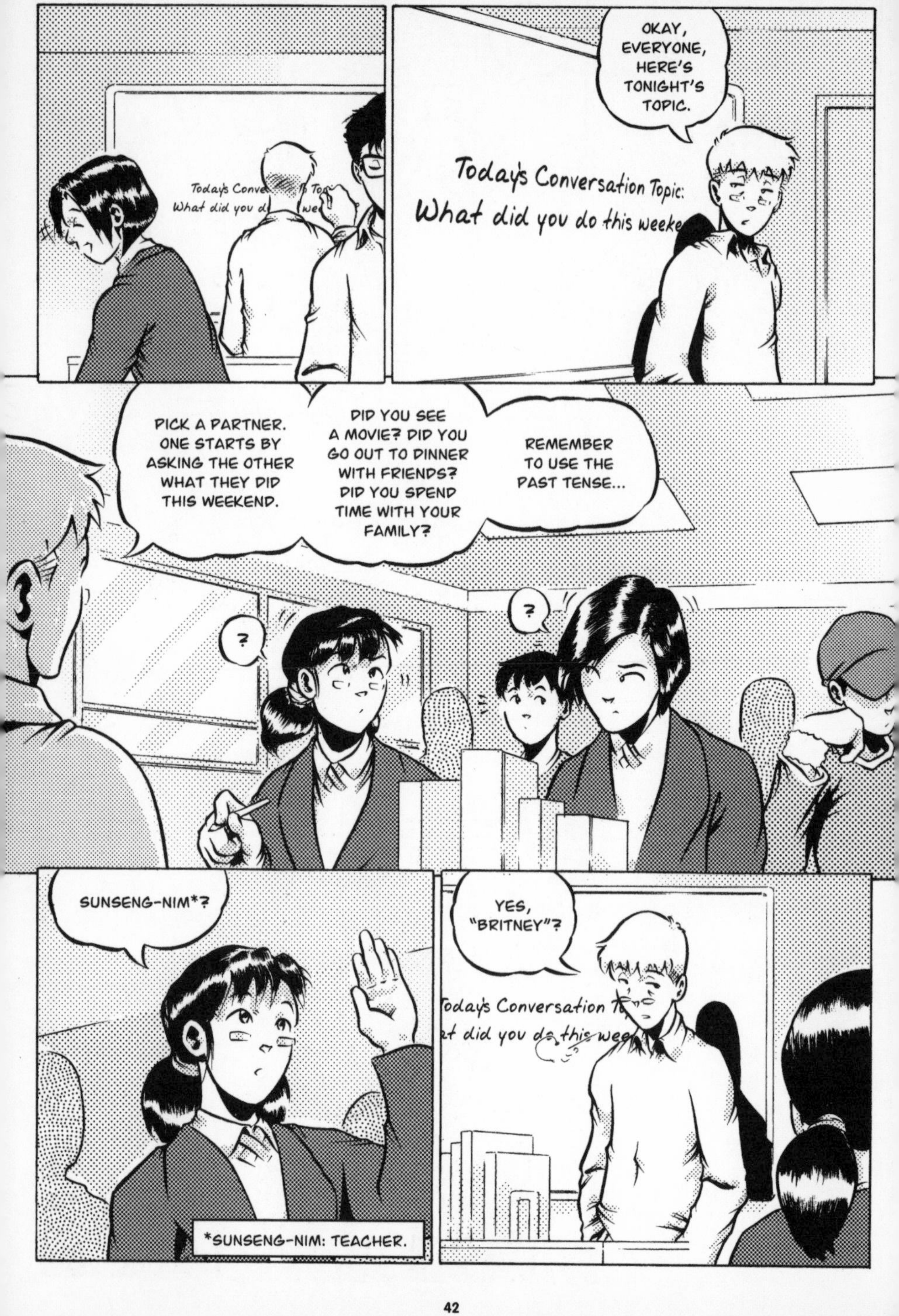
Today's Conversation Topic: What did you do this weekend
OKAY, EVERYONE, HERE'S TONIGHT'S TOPIC.
PICK A PARTNER. ONE STARTS BY ASKING THE OTHER WHAT THEY DID THIS WEEKEND.
DID YOU SEE A MOVIE? DID YOU GO OUT TO DINNER WITH FRIENDS? DID YOU SPEND TIME WITH YOUR FAMILY?
REMEMBER TO USE THE PAST TENSE...
?
?
SUNSENG-NIM*?
YES, "BRITNEY"?
*SUNSENG-NIM: TEACHER.

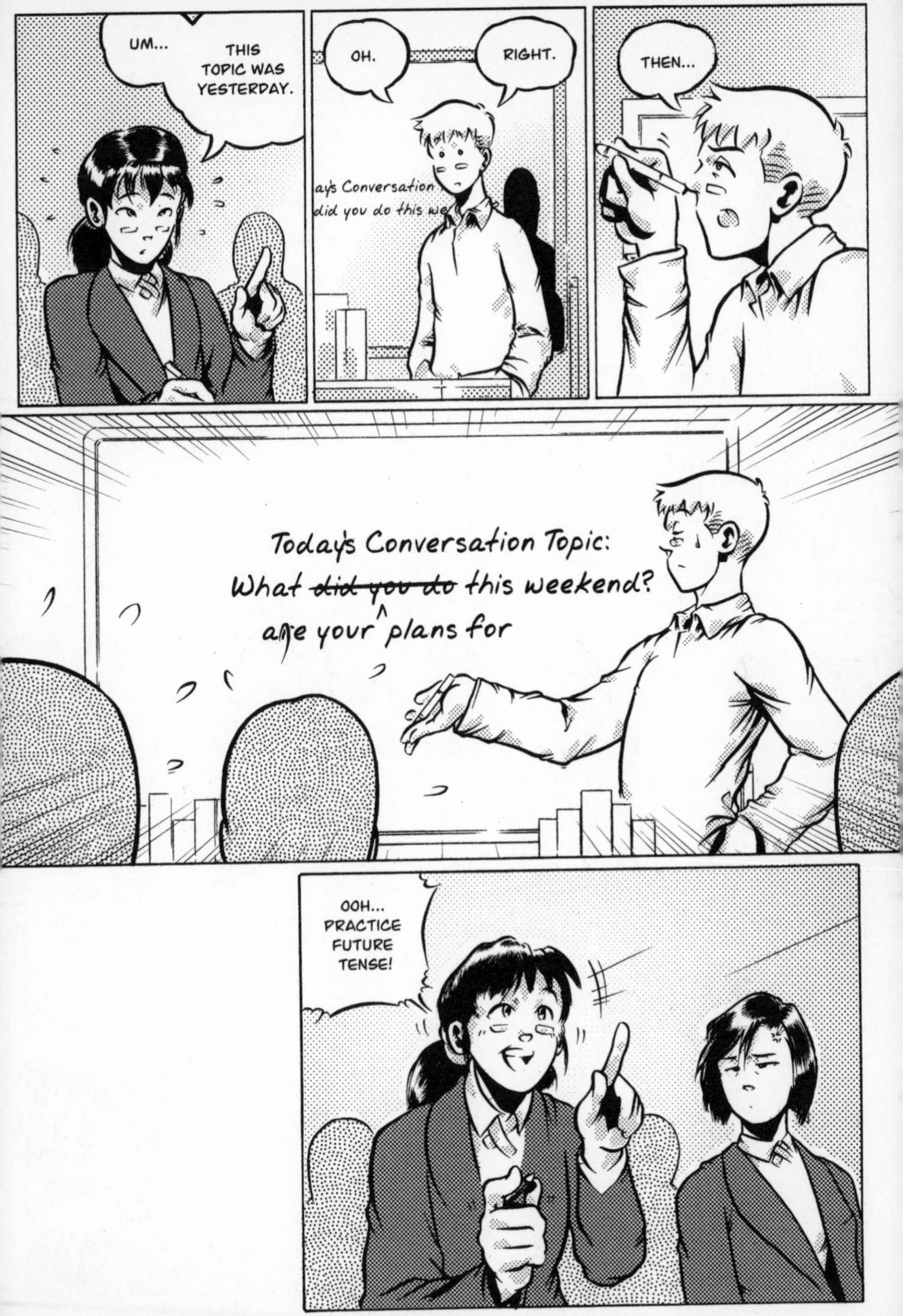
UM...
THIS TOPIC WAS YESTERDAY.
OH.
RIGHT.
THEN...
Today's Conversation Topic:
What ~~did you do~~ this weekend?
are your plans for
OOH... PRACTICE FUTURE TENSE!

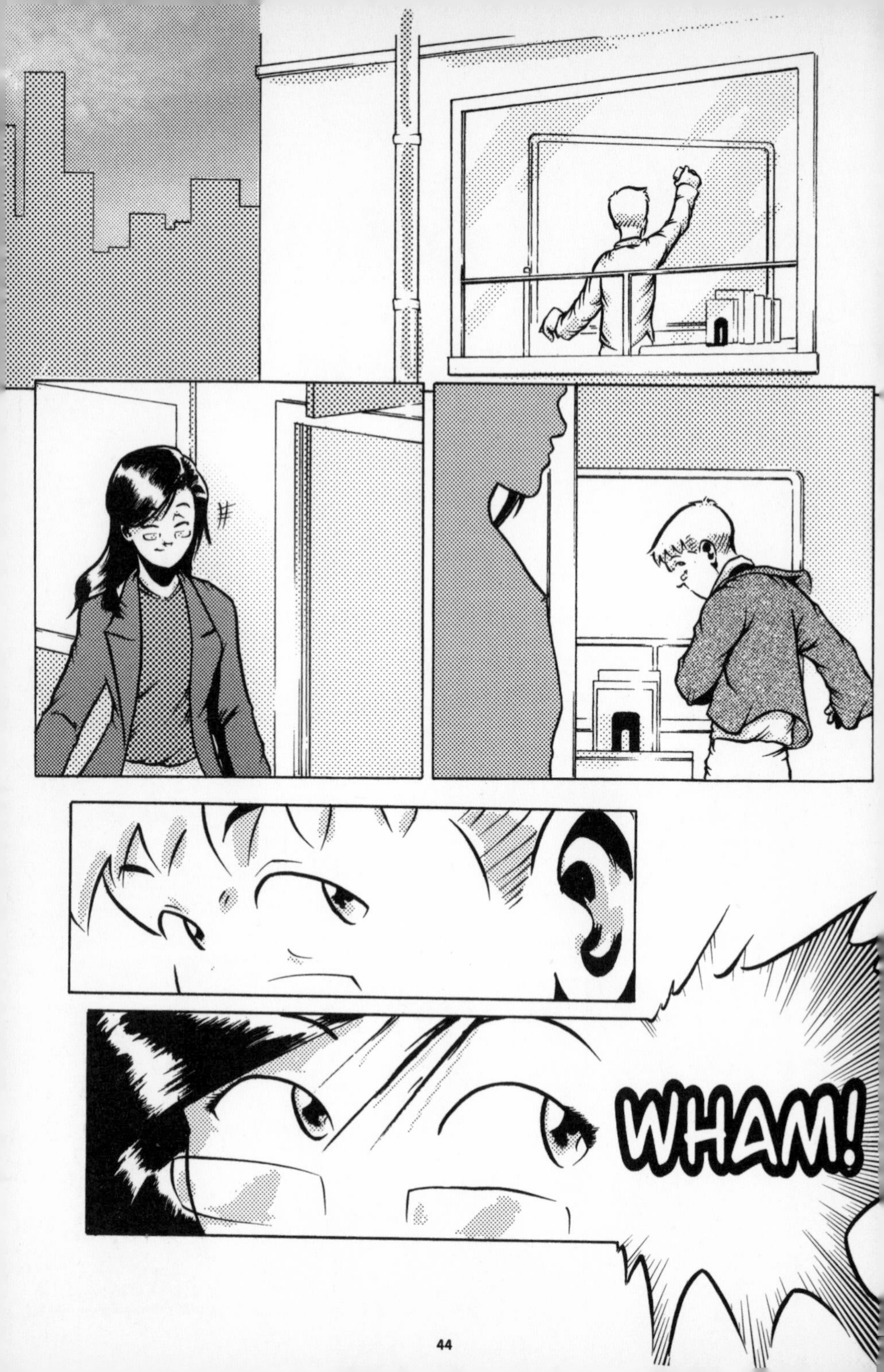
WHAM!

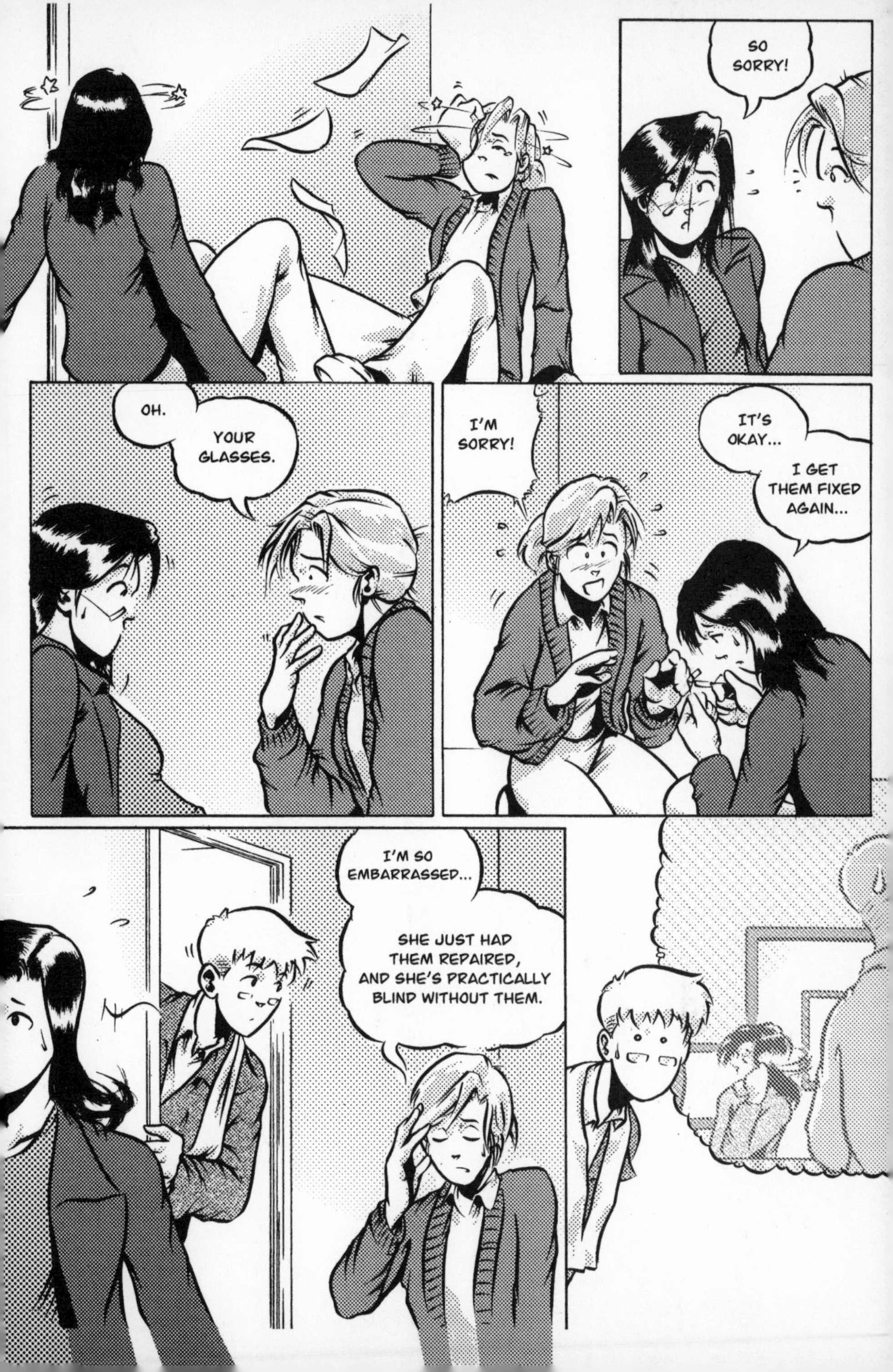
SO SORRY!
OH.
YOUR GLASSES.
I'M SORRY!
IT'S OKAY...
I GET THEM FIXED AGAIN...
I'M SO EMBARRASSED...
SHE JUST HAD THEM REPAIRED, AND SHE'S PRACTICALLY BLIND WITHOUT THEM.

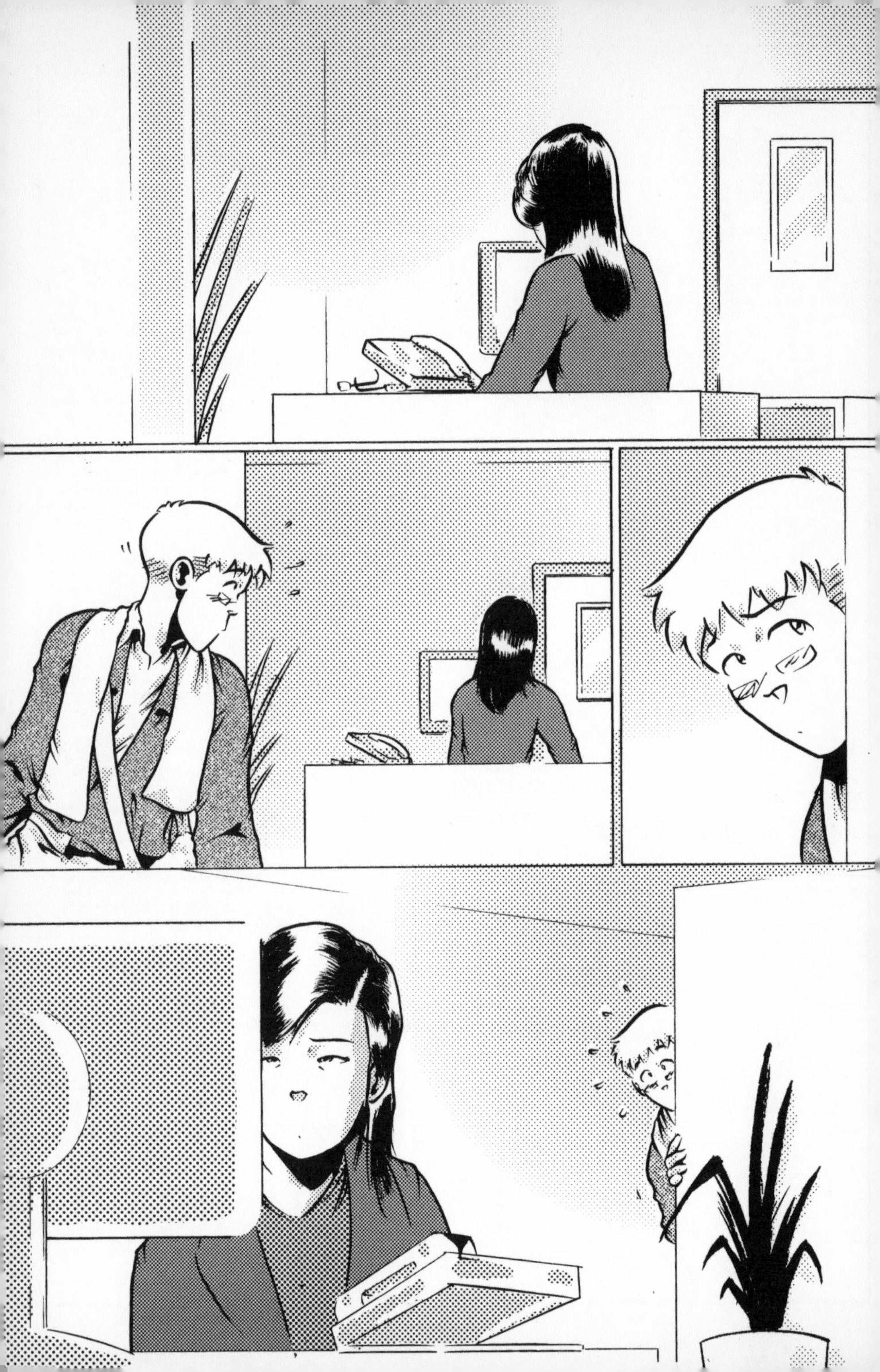

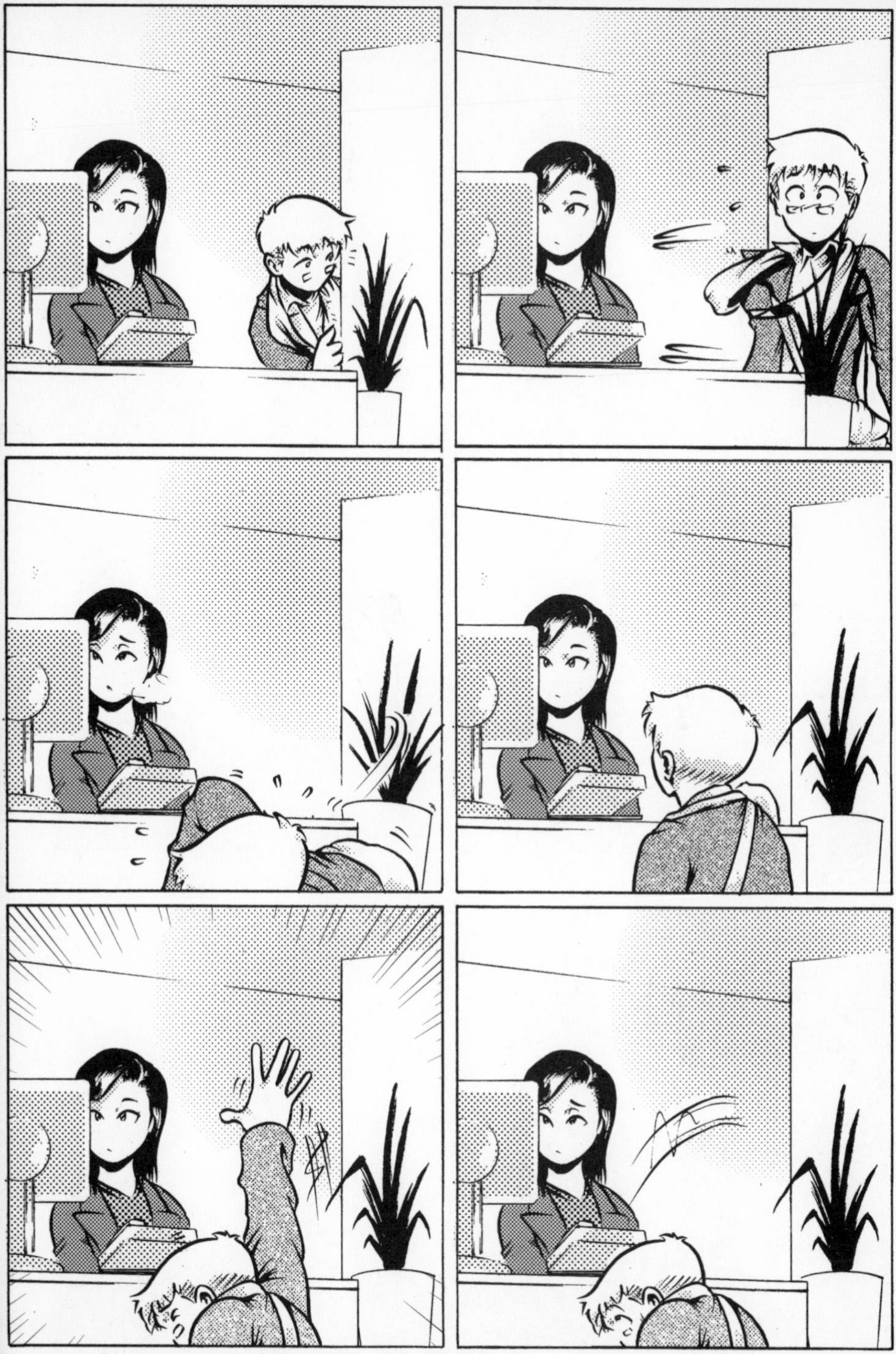

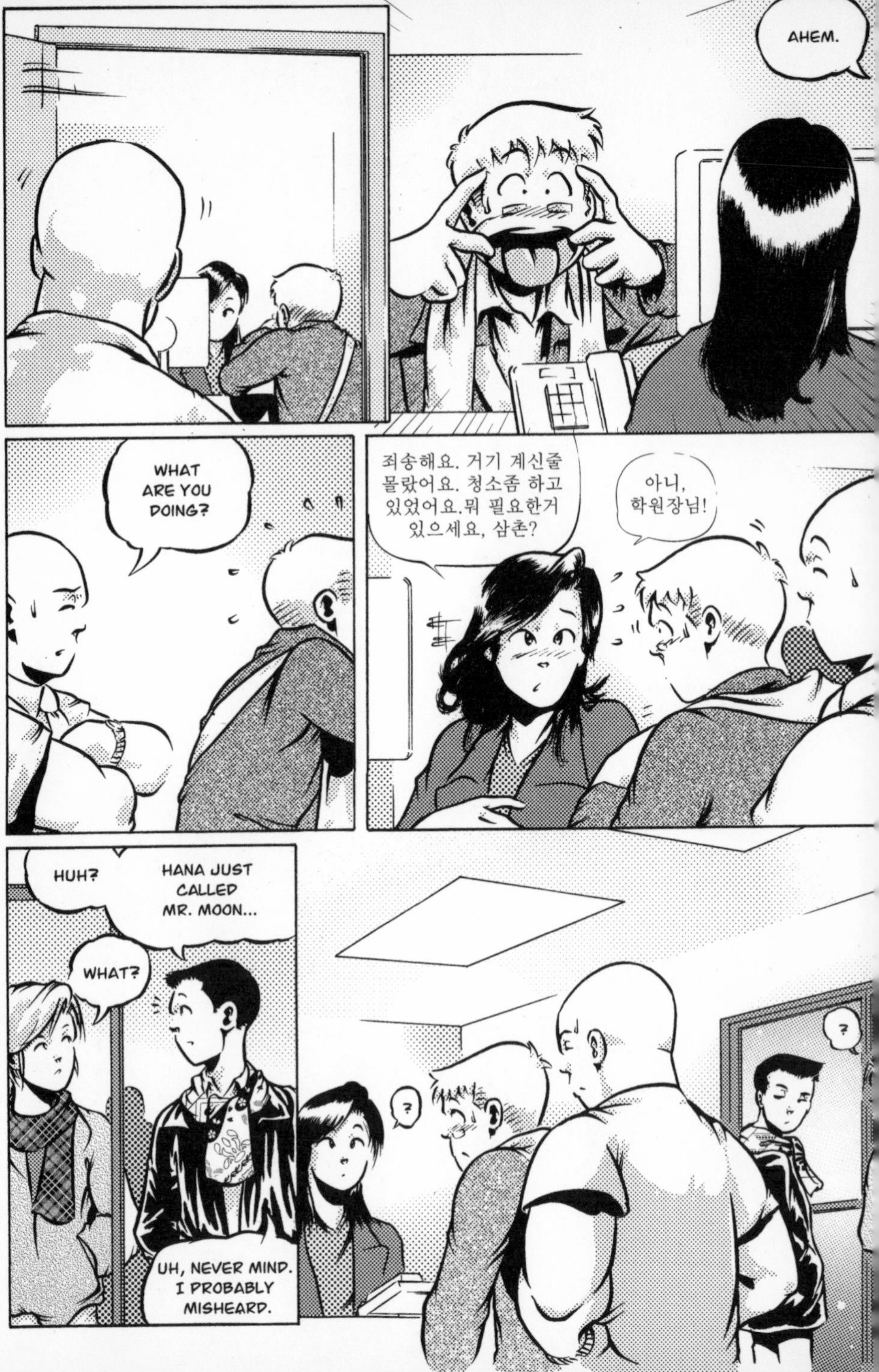
AHEM.
WHAT ARE YOU DOING?
죄송해요. 거기 계신줄 몰랐어요. 청소좀 하고 있었어요.뭐 필요한거 있으세요, 삼촌?
아니, 학원장님!
HUH?
HANA JUST CALLED MR. MOON...
WHAT?
?
?
UH, NEVER MIND. I PROBABLY MISHEARD.

Chapter 18

KING KONGLISH

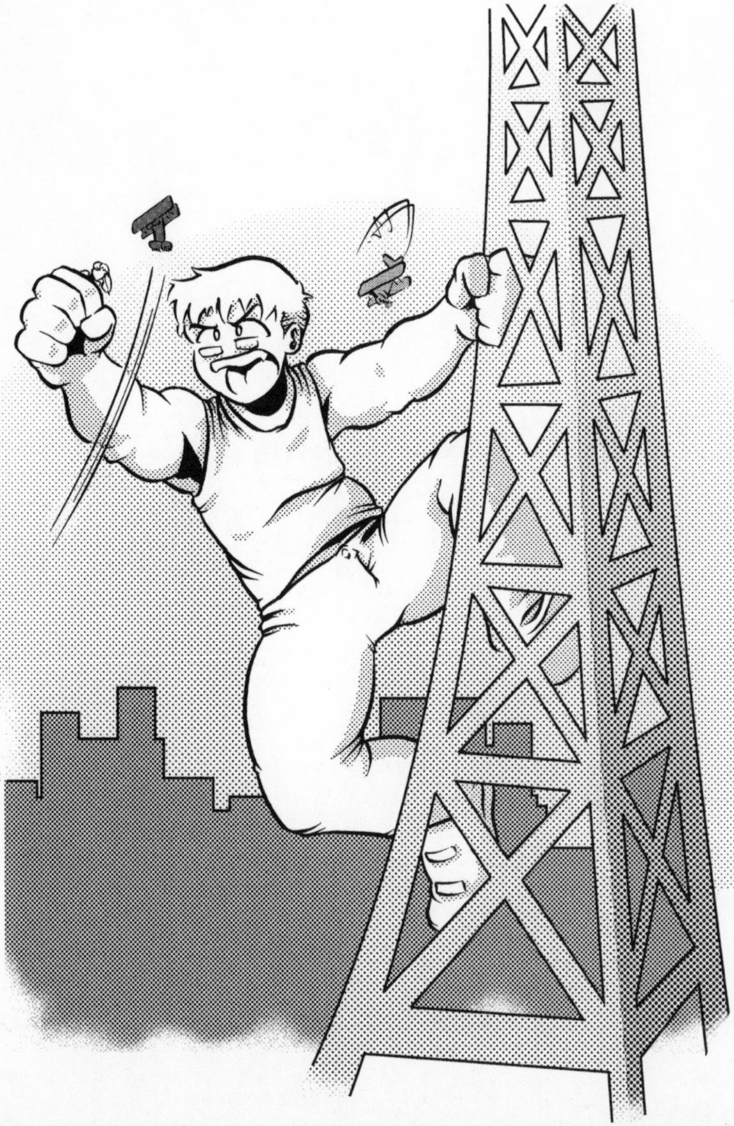

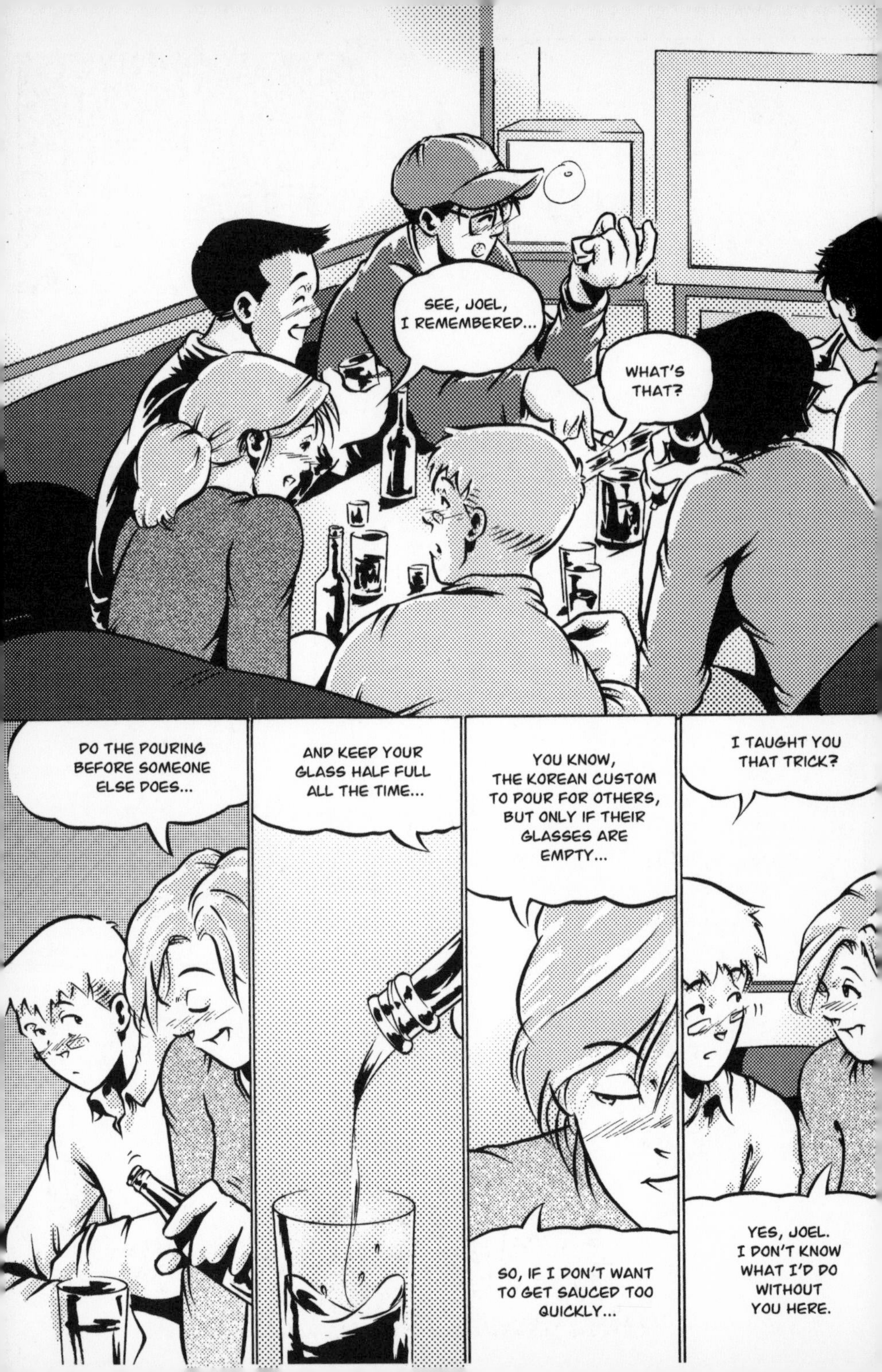
SEE, JOEL, I REMEMBERED...
WHAT'S THAT?
DO THE POURING BEFORE SOMEONE ELSE DOES...
AND KEEP YOUR GLASS HALF FULL ALL THE TIME...
YOU KNOW, THE KOREAN CUSTOM TO POUR FOR OTHERS, BUT ONLY IF THEIR GLASSES ARE EMPTY...
SO, IF I DON'T WANT TO GET SAUCED TOO QUICKLY...
I TAUGHT YOU THAT TRICK?
YES, JOEL. I DON'T KNOW WHAT I'D DO WITHOUT YOU HERE.

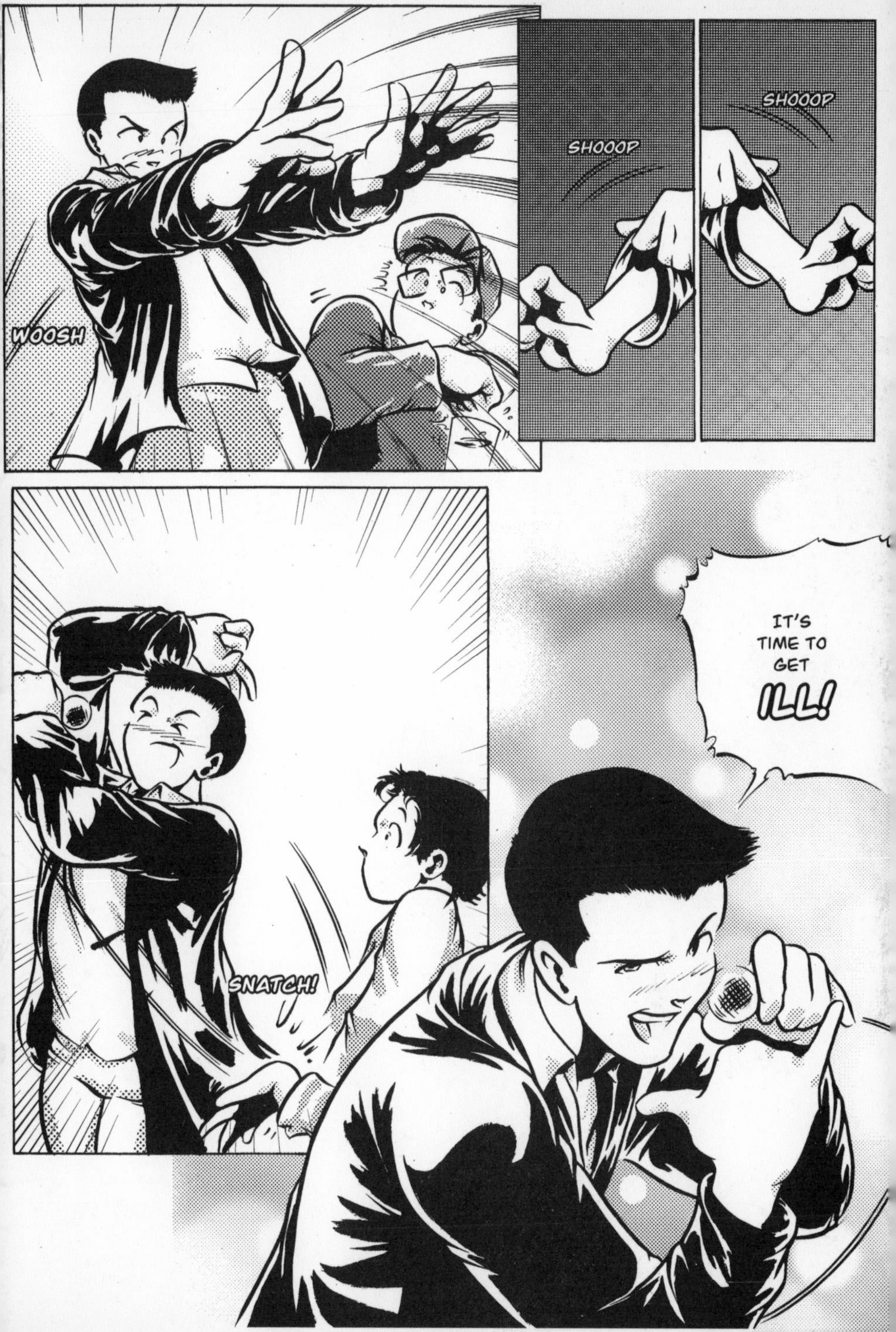
WOOSH
SHOOOP
SHOOOP
SNATCH!
IT'S TIME TO GET ILL!

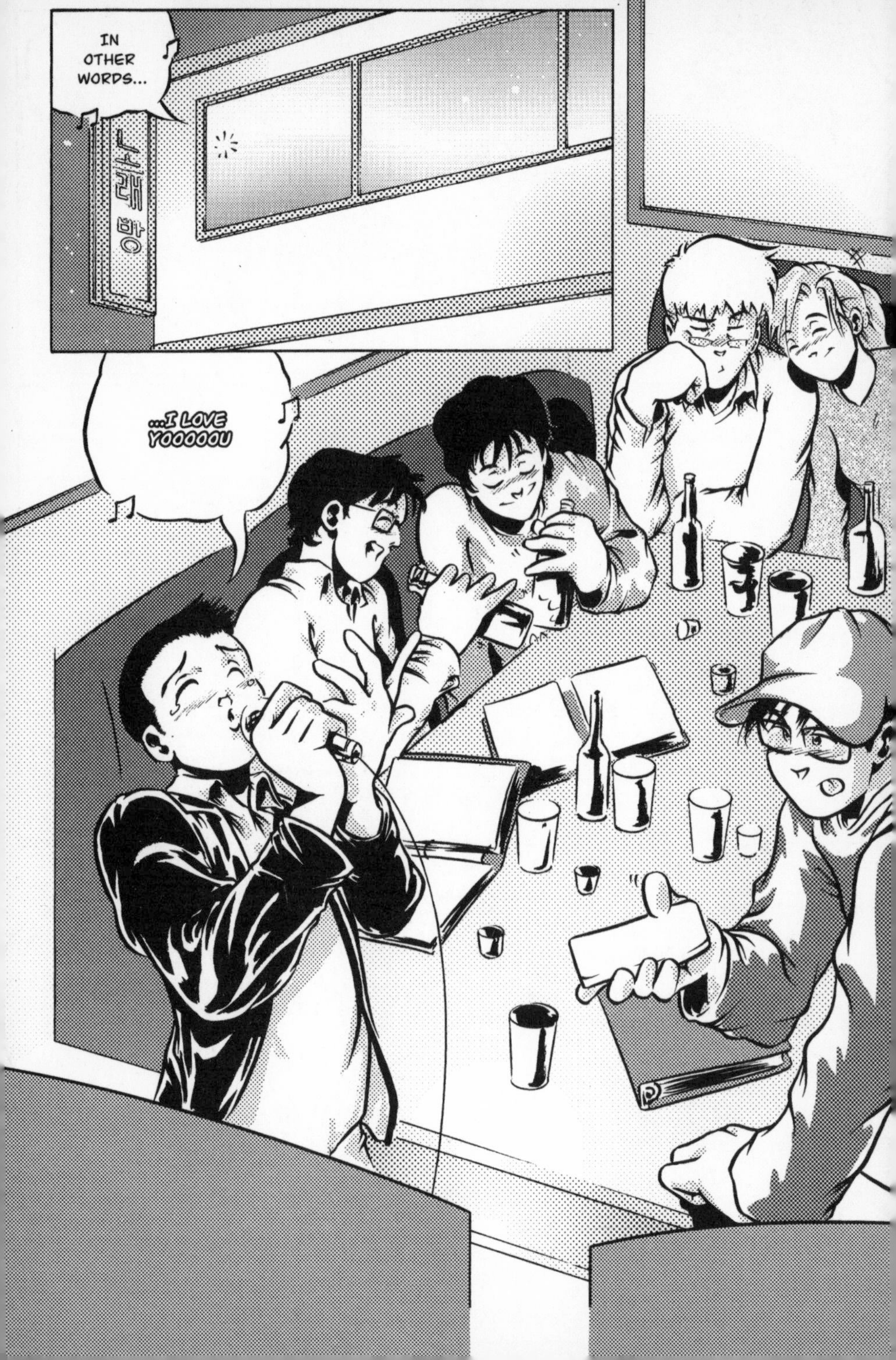
IN OTHER WORDS...
노래방
...I LOVE YOOOOOU

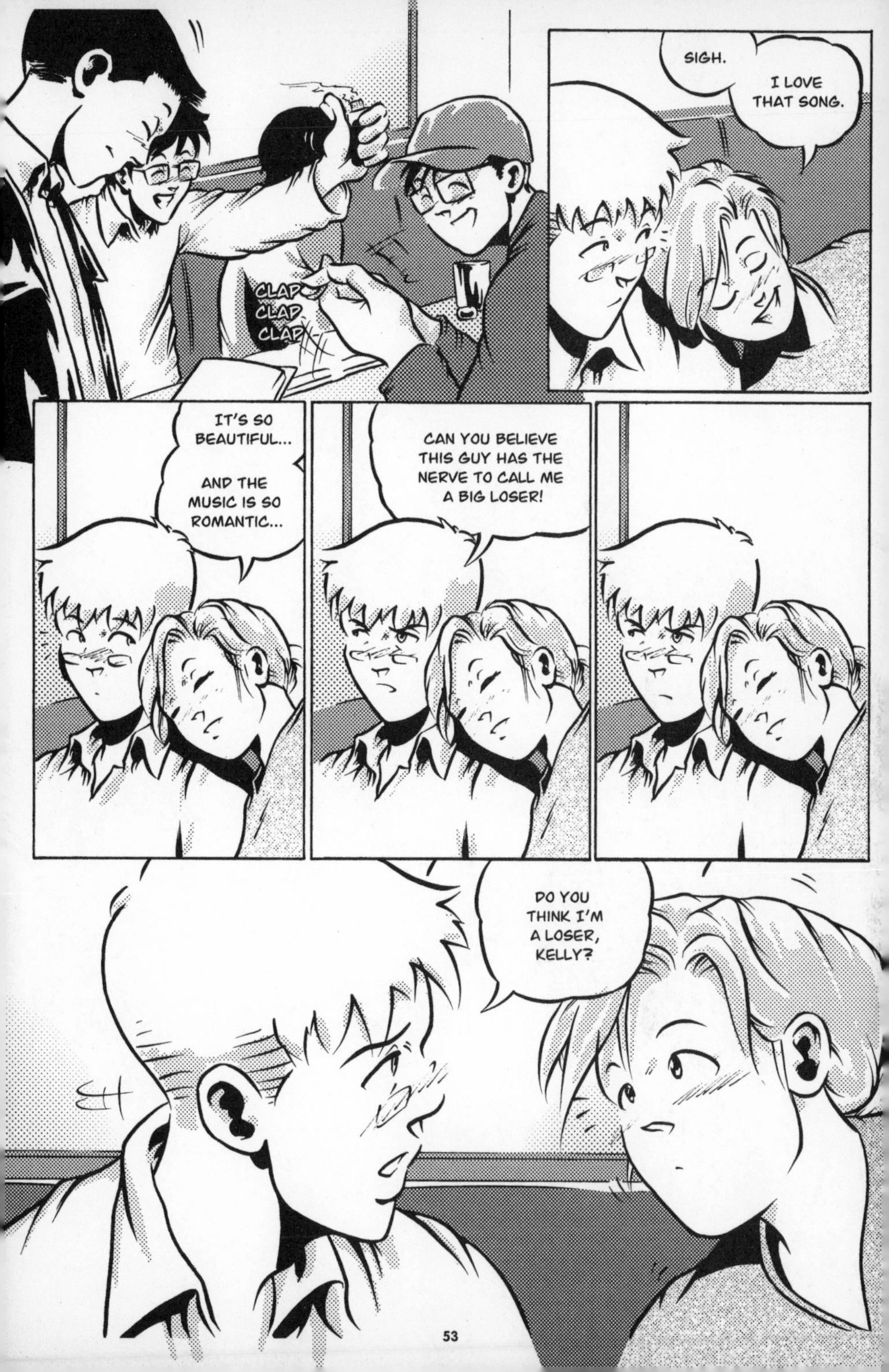
CLAP
CLAP
CLAP
SIGH.
I LOVE THAT SONG.
IT'S SO BEAUTIFUL...
AND THE MUSIC IS SO ROMANTIC...
CAN YOU BELIEVE THIS GUY HAS THE NERVE TO CALL ME A BIG LOSER!
DO YOU THINK I'M A LOSER, KELLY?

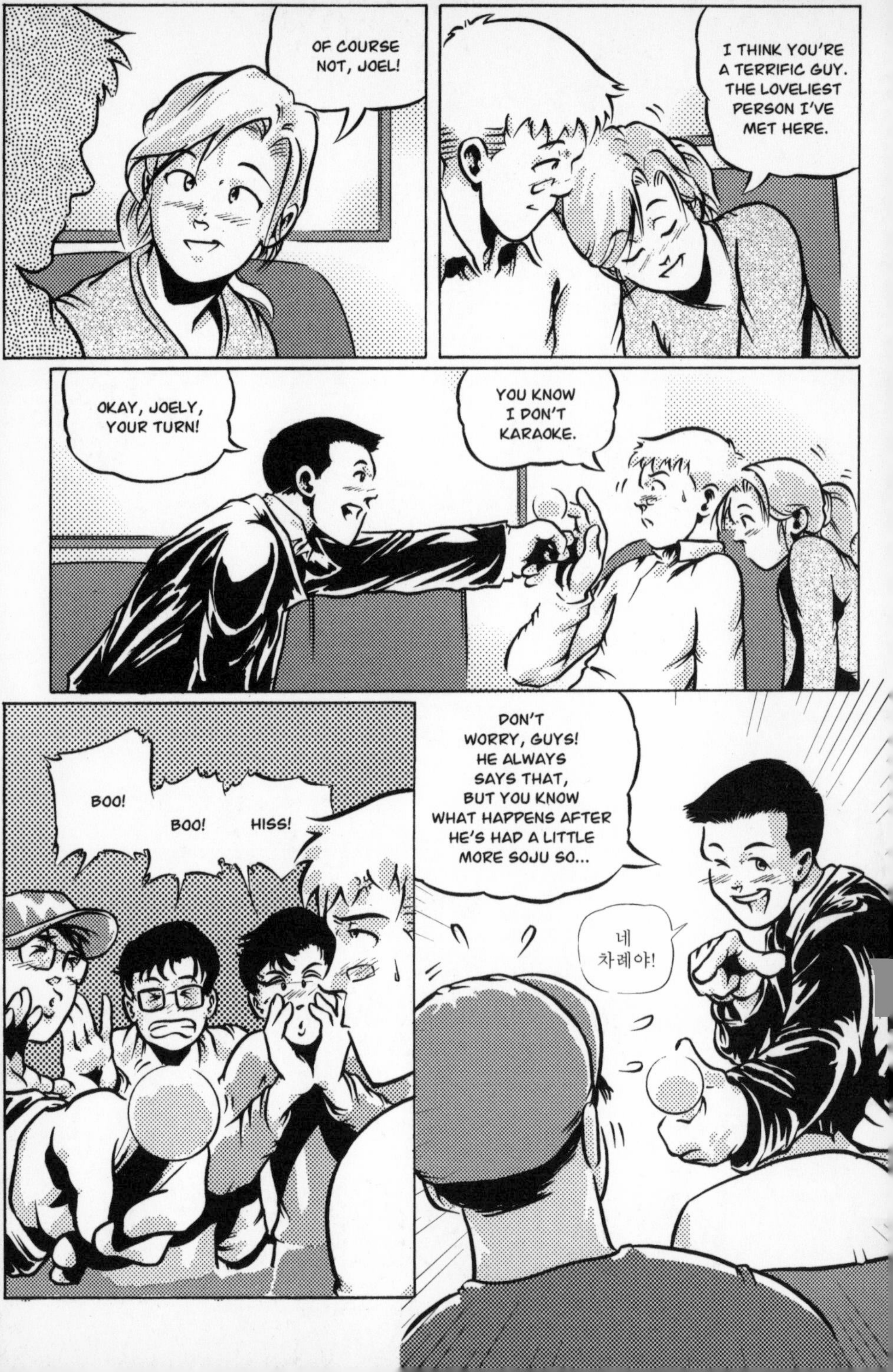
OF COURSE NOT, JOEL!
I THINK YOU'RE A TERRIFIC GUY. THE LOVELIEST PERSON I'VE MET HERE.
OKAY, JOELY, YOUR TURN!
YOU KNOW I DON'T KARAOKE.
BOO!
BOO!
HISS!
DON'T WORRY, GUYS! HE ALWAYS SAYS THAT, BUT YOU KNOW WHAT HAPPENS AFTER HE'S HAD A LITTLE MORE SOJU SO...
네 차례야!

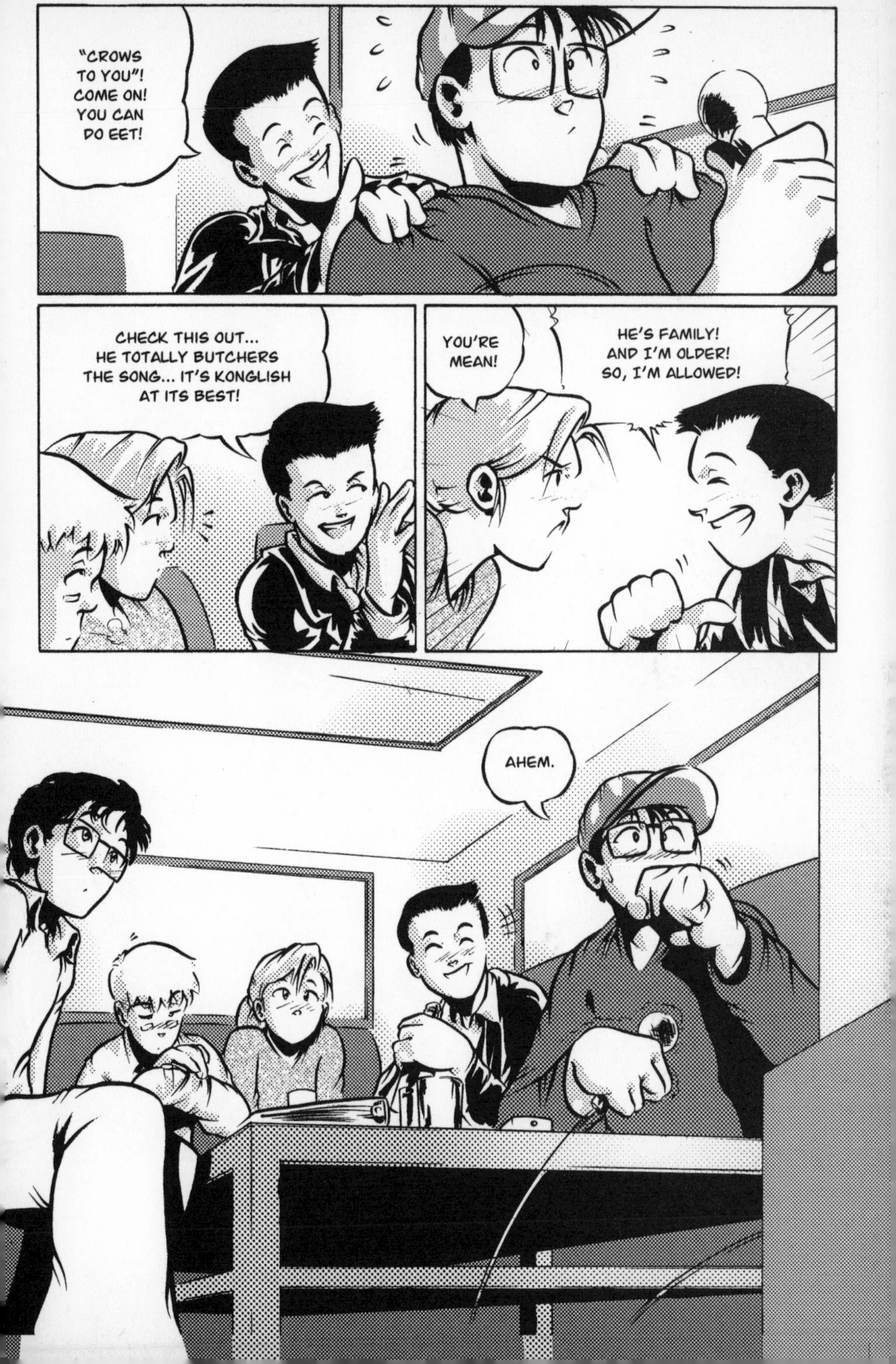
"CROWS TO YOU"! COME ON! YOU CAN DO EET!
CHECK THIS OUT... HE TOTALLY BUTCHERS THE SONG... IT'S KONGLISH AT ITS BEST!
YOU'RE MEAN!
HE'S FAMILY! AND I'M OLDER! SO, I'M ALLOWED!
AHEM.

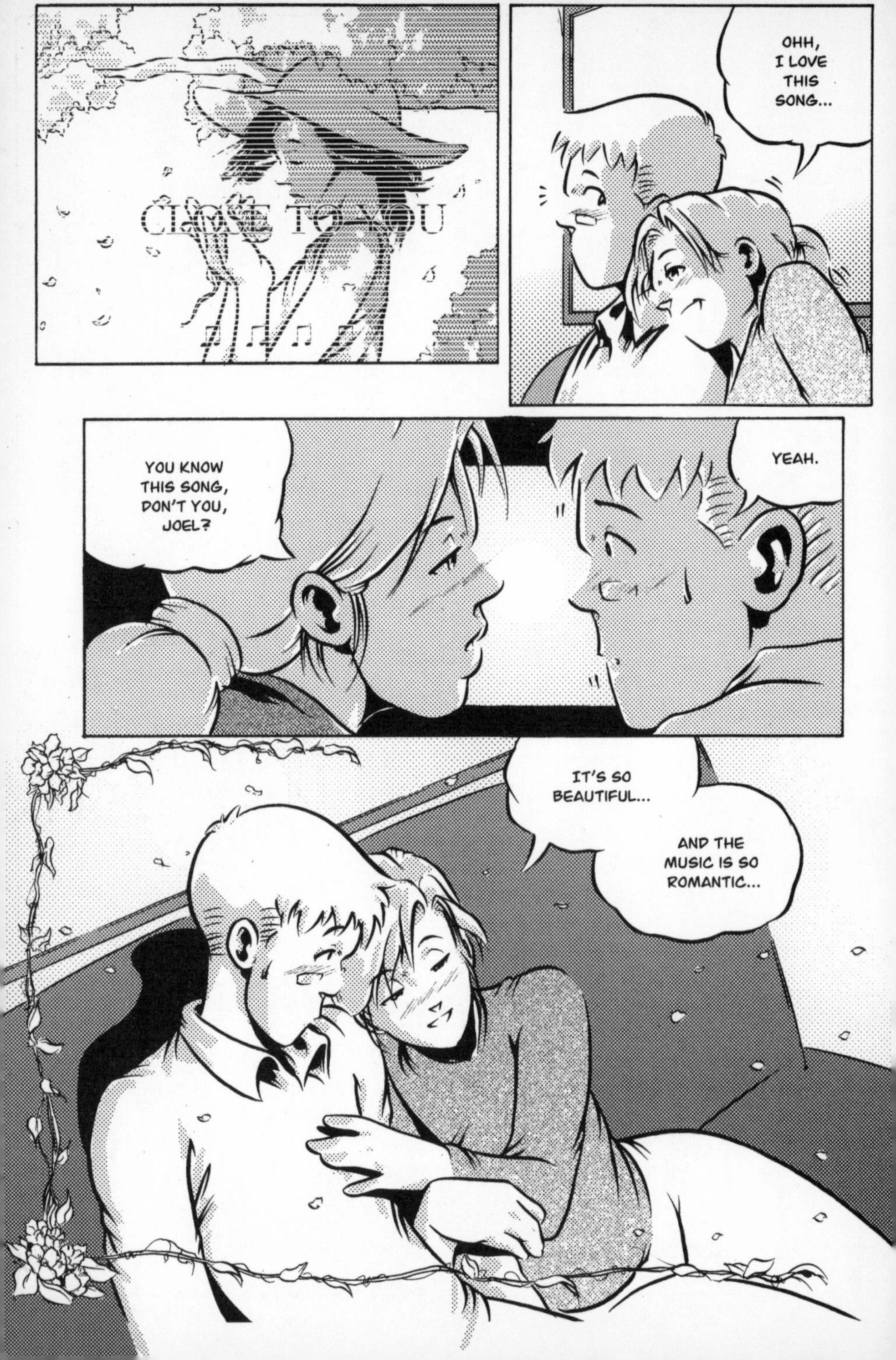
CLOSE TO YOU
OHH, I LOVE THIS SONG...
YOU KNOW THIS SONG, DON'T YOU, JOEL?
YEAH.
IT'S SO BEAUTIFUL...
AND THE MUSIC IS SO ROMANTIC...

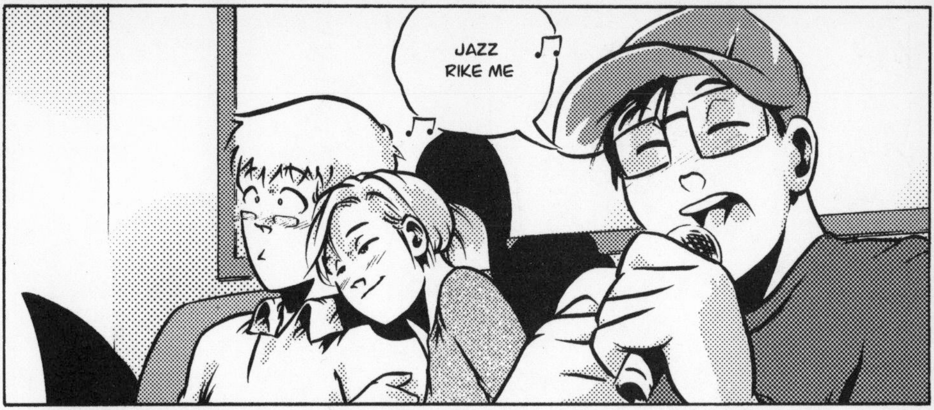
JAZZ
RIKE ME

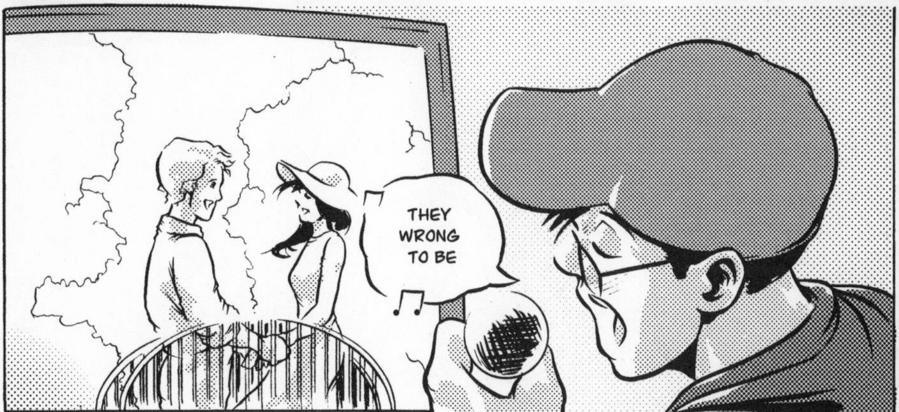
THEY
WRONG
TO BE

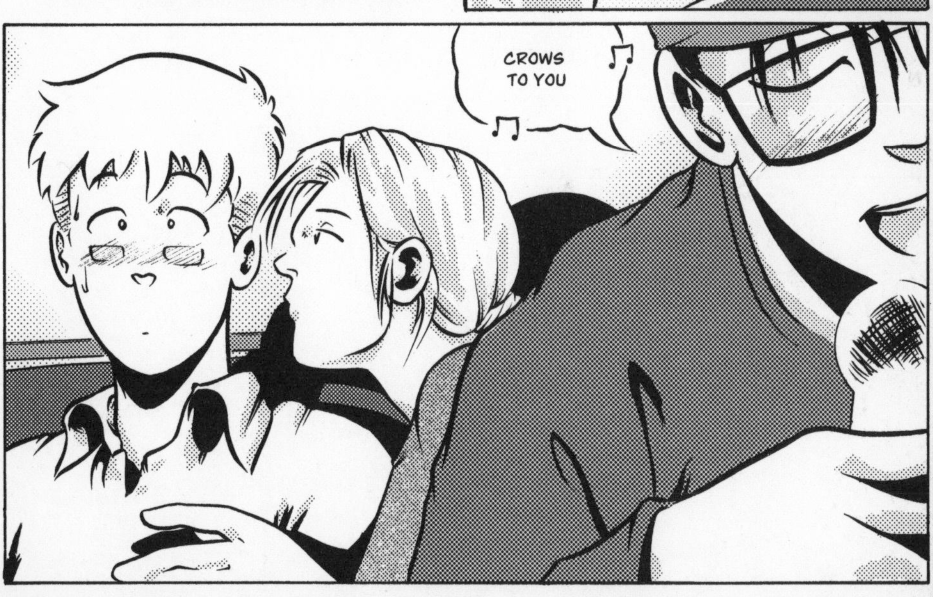
CROWS
TO YOU

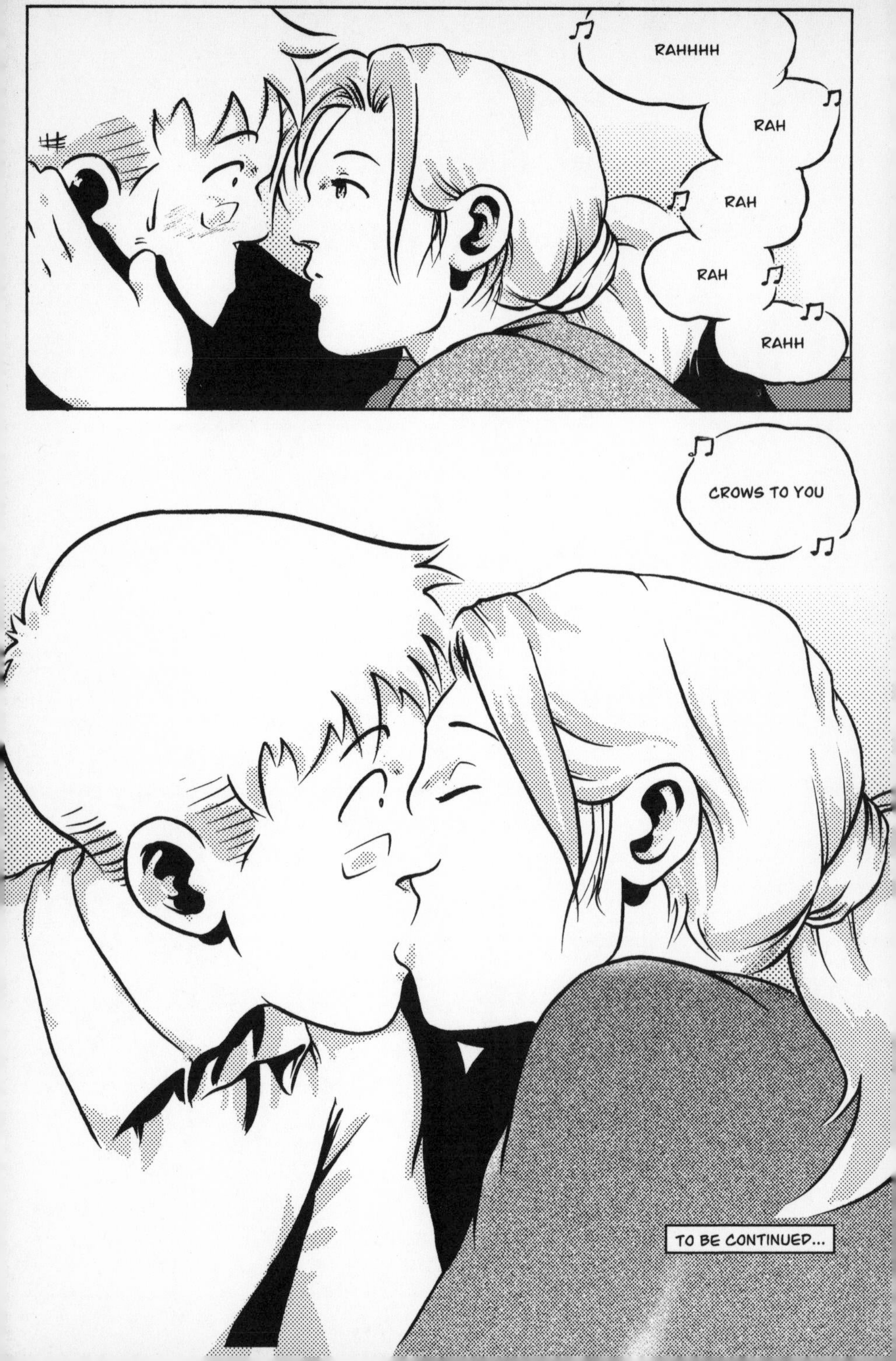
RAHHHH
RAH
RAH
RAH
RAHH
CROWS TO YOU
TO BE CONTINUED...

LOST IN TRANSLATION
Or
WHAT ARE THESE PEOPLE SAYING, ANYWAY?

PAGE 20

Panel 5

COUSIN: THAT WAS… BEAUTIFUL.

PAGE 29

Panel 5

MR. LEE: HAVE YOU EATEN?

PAGE 48

Panel 4

HANA: SORRY, I DID NOT SEE YOU THERE. I WAS JUST TIDYING UP. DID YOU NEED SOMETHING, UNCLE?

HANA: I MEAN, MR. MOON!

PAGE 54

Panel 5

DONNIE: YOUR TURN!

OTHER BOOKS BY J. TORRES...

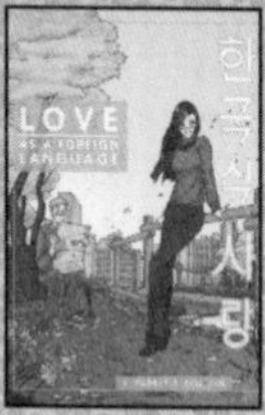
LOVE
AS A FOREIGN LANGUAGE

LOVE AS A FOREIGN LANGUAGE 1
by J. Torres & Eric Kim
72 pages, black-and-white interiors
$5.95 US
ISBN 1-932664-06-8

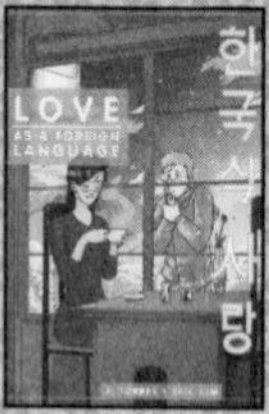
LOVE
AS A FOREIGN LANGUAGE

LOVE AS A FOREIGN LANGUAGE 2
by J. Torres & Eric Kim
72 pages, black-and-white interiors
$5.95 US
ISBN 1-932664-06-8

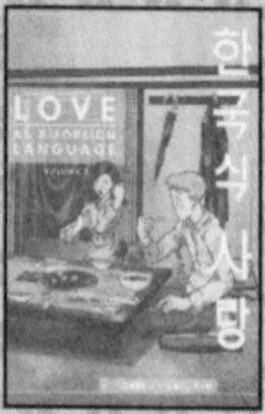
LOVE
AS A FOREIGN LANGUAGE

LOVE AS A FOREIGN LANGUAGE 3
by J. Torres & Eric Kim
72 pages, black-and-white interiors
$5.95 US
ISBN 1-932664-18-1

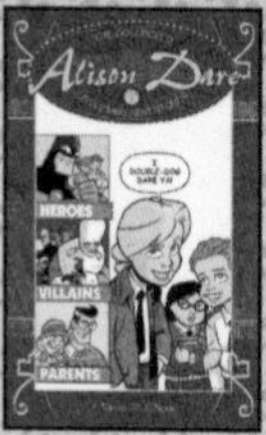
Alison Dare
HEROES
VILLAINS
PARENTS

ALISON DARE™, VOLUME 1
illustrated by J. Bone
104 pages
black-and-white interiors
$8.95 US
ISBN 1-929998-20-1

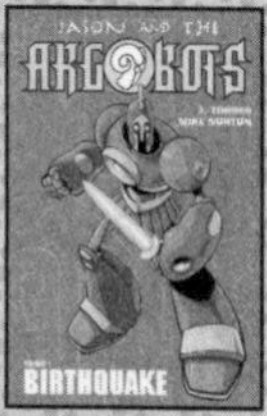
JASON AND THE
ARGOBOTS
BIRTHQUAKE

JASON & THE ARGOBOTS™,
VOLUME 1: BIRTHQUAKE
illustrated by Mike Norton
120 pages
black-and-white interiors
$11.95 US
ISBN 1-929998-55-4

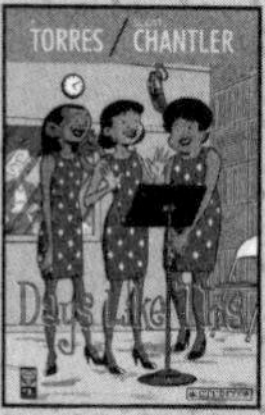
TORRES / CHANTLER

DAYS LIKE THIS™
illustrated by Scott Chantler
88 pages
black-and-white interiors
$8.95 US
ISBN 1-929998-48-1

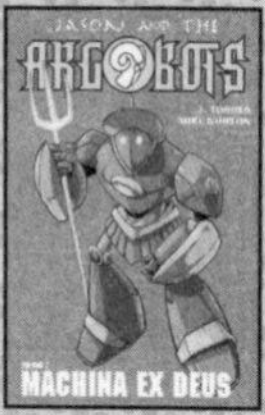
JASON AND THE
ARGOBOTS
MACHINA EX DEUS

JASON & THE ARGOBOTS™
VOLUME 2: MACHINA EX DEUS
illustrated by Mike Norton
120 pages
black-and-white interiors
$11.95 US
ISBN 1-929998-56-2

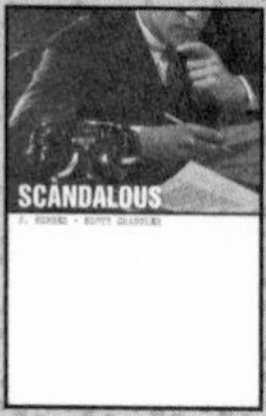
SCANDALOUS

SCANDALOUS™
illustrated by Scott Chantler
104 pages
black-and-white interiors
$9.95 US
ISBN 1-929998-98-8

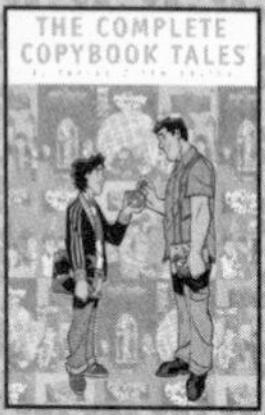
THE COMPLETE
COPYBOOK TALES

THE COMPLETE COPYBOOK TALES ™
illustrated by Tim Levins
with Jeff Wasson
240 pages
black-and-white interiors
$19.95 US
ISBN 1-929998-20-1

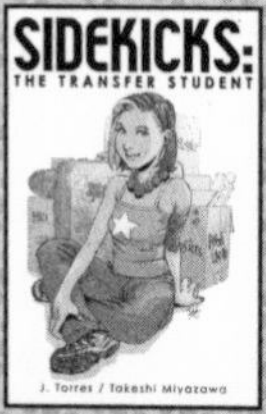
SIDEKICKS:
THE TRANSFER STUDENT
J. Torres / Takeshi Miyazawa

SIDEKICKS™:
THE TRANSFER STUDENT
illustrated by Takeshi Miyazawa
104 pages
black-and-white interiors
$11.95 US
ISBN 1-929998-76-7

Available at finer comics shops everywhere. For a comics store near you, call 1-888-COMIC-BOOK or visit www.the-master-list.com.

For more Oni Press titles and information visit www.onipress.com.